FARMING IS A FUNNY BUSINESS

A COLLECTION OF FARMING JOKES AND ANECDOTES

COMPILED BY

JOHN AND ANDREW ARBUCKLE

SOLD IN AID OF RSABI

financial assistance · support · helpline

for

agriculture · forestry · fish farming · rural estate work · gamekeeping · crofting · horticulture

tel: 0300 111 4166 | www.rsabi.org.uk | Scottish Charity No. SC009828

SCOTLAND'S CHARITY HELPING PEOPLE WHO HAVE DEPENDED ON THE LAND

Published in 2015 by RSABI
Rural Centre
West Mains
Ingliston
Midlothian
EH28 8LT

ISBN: 978-0-9928090-1-0

British Library Cataloguing-in-Publication Data
A catalogue record for this book is available on request from the
British Library.

Designed and typeset by Polaris Publishing, Edinburgh

www.polarispublishing.com

Printed by
The Printing House
3rd Floor,
14 Hanover Street
London W1S 1YH

A MESSAGE FROM RSABI

Have you ever heard the one about the NFU Scotland President who lost his phone on a nudist beach in Portugal? Or the CEO with an uncanny ability to set things on fire? What about the EU Commissioner who rearranged the seating plans at a dinner in Edinburgh Castle ....

We farmers are often thought of as dour but as this book proves that is not the case. Even when times are tough, for whatever reason, we manage to keep our sense of humour.

Welcome to this collection of humorous agricultural anecdotes and jokes from Scotland's farmers and those from the associated trades. Our thanks go to the many individual contributors with a special thanks to Andrew and John Arbuckle who painstakingly collated the material.

All funds from the sale of this book will be donated to RSABI. Rest assured the money will be used wisely to further the aims of RSABI.

Above all else enjoy reading this – you may even be in it –and a special thanks for buying it.

Nina Clancy CEO RSABI & John Kinnaird Chairman RSABI

rsabi

Help us, help them.

Join our Supporters Scheme

Supporter Scheme 2015

0300 111 4166

www.rsabi.org.uk

Scottish Charity Number: SC009828

rsabi

RSABI is a unique Scottish Charity with roots going back to 1897.

Every year RSABI helps hundreds of people who have worked in land-based industries.

RSABI provides financial assistance, support, and a helpline.

To find out more about RSABI, please visit our website at www.rsabi.org.uk

Contact us at The Rural centre,
West Mains of Ingliston, Newbridge,
Edinburgh EH28 8LT
Tel 0300 111 4166
Email rsabi@rsabi.org.uk

Follow us on Facebook using
www.facebook.com/RSABI.ORG where you will
find "up to the minute" information on regional
events and how you can get involved.

Find us on Twitter @RSABI for news and
information.

ALSO BY ANDREW ARBUCKLE

Footsteps in the Furrow
We waved to the Baker
Sparks from the Smiddy

AND BY JOHN AND ANDREW ARBUCKLE

The First One Hundred Years – the story of NFU Scotland

THANKS

To all those who sent in stories. Where there were duplicates we used the simple formula of first submission counted.

To the cartoonists. Brian Petrie and Graham Lang

Although a cartoonist for over twenty years, Brian's first job was tattie howking at Kincraigie and Drumdreel farms during his primary school days in Strathmiglo.

It was obvious this was never going to be a permanent position, so a stint studying graphic design in Edinburgh was followed by twenty odd years in the Art dept of DC Thomson in Dundee. In 1995 Brian packed his bags and started a new career as a cartoonist, working for *The Sunday Mail* and *The Scottish Sun*. Earlier this year he won Cartoonist of the year at the Scottish Press Awards after two decades of trying.

Graham Lang, after a successful career in business, is now well known for his humorous, tongue in cheek, pen and ink drawings illustrating incidents in shooting, fishing and golf. He has an occasional foray into political satire poking fun at the Scottish Government and the wind farm industry. His portrait caricatures adorn many walls in Scotland and further afield. He is delighted to be supporting the RSABI through this book on the funny side of farming.

Thank you all.

INTRODUCTION

John and Andrew Arbuckle

When John and I hatched up a plan to put together a book of funny stories about farming and rural life, it all seemed so simple. We had both lived and worked in agriculture for a long number of years and during that time, we had, even in the toughest times, seen and heard a great deal of humour. Some of it was, of the moment, often when a piece of machinery broke down or some of the farm livestock either escaped or became ill or even died.

So we knew the funny incidents were there, it was only a question of digging them out. This delving was most enjoyable with contribution from all over the country plus several from Scots now living in Australia. Some came in singly, others in batches. Some were too rude to print but most were just fine. Some stories were obviously old friends well-polished in their keeping.

Several reactions can be predicted. The first is "I have heard that story before." We have also heard a number of the jokes and anecdotes on previous occasions but after testing them on unsuspecting friends, we decided that not everybody knew them and they should be included. Some funny stories have a long life. One of our prolific contributors, Jim Webster, Dunkeld, recalled performing in a concert party in the mid 1970s. The venue was the BLESMA home for war veterans in Crieff. After the show one old soldier ushered him over to tell Jim that he had first heard one of his jokes when serving in the trenches in the First World War. Without giving the game away, the story in question admittedly disguised a little appears in this volume one hundred years on. Those who submitted the recycled stories make no claim to their origin and are credited only with their contribution.

Another prediction is that, after reading the book, some readers will claim to know better funnier stories. That may well be true but it does bring to mind the observation by the late Matt Mundell that every farmer standing around the judging ring believes he/she has superior stock at home. Anyone wishing to demonstrate their stories are better can send them to us and we might do a follow up book next year.

A third certainty is that some people will laugh uproariously at some of the contributions while their neighbours will frown and wonder where is the humour in the tale? We are all different and to cater for this diversity, we have included a range of jokes and personal anecdotes.

Linger no longer on this introduction. Read on but, in similar fashion to eating a Christmas cake, do not attempt to devour it all at one sitting.

WARNING

There are thirteen chapters in the book. Each contains a mixture of jokes and anecdotes. We originally were going to parcel them up under differing headings such as 'Salesmen' or 'loons or halfins' but then we decided one of the joys of funny stories is their diversity.

Thus, in your reading, you will jump effortlessly from a story about crofting to a political anecdote. We hope you enjoy the variety.

ONE

A farmer sees a collie tied to a post at a farm sale. A notice next to it said, "Talking dog for sale. Ring my mobile. I'm here at the sale." The farmer looks around to see if anyone is looking, then he says to the collie, "I hear you can talk, say something about yourself."

"Well," said the dog, "last week I advised Richard Lochhead on a new IT system, and sorted the old one. Then I swam the length of Loch Ness and raised £75k for RSABI. Then I coached Andy Murray for a few sessions when he needed some extra help for Wimbledon."

The farmer looks amazed.

The sale takes place and the farmer pays £5,000 for the rare dog and as he leads it away, the owner seemed unusually pleased. The farmer asked inquiringly, "Why on earth do you want to sell this amazing beast?"

"It was the lies I couldn't take," he said and walked away.

Aileen Orr, Paxton

Many good friendships were forged when NFUS Council meetings alternated between Edinburgh and Glasgow. Quite often we in Banffshire went down the night before to try and do some good work prior to the actual meeting. Somehow the Banffshire men seemed to outlast them all at these late nights; redoubtable men such as Willie Fraser of Glenlivet of whom it was said, the more he had, the taller he stood and he was 6ft to start with. The only way they got these characters to bed was when they put the price of a nip up to £1.50.

Alan Meldrum, formerly NFUS Banff

Years ago Jim Lawrie, Cuthill Towers, Milnathort was taking his caravan to the Highland Show when the police waved him down. "Do you realise you were speeding?" asked the officer. Jim still in his dungarees, replied, "The fairmer just told me to go and deliver this caravan and I had no idea o' the power of this car." The policeman eased back and said, "When you get back home, tell your boss he has to warn you about the dangers of speeding."

George Lawrie, NFUS treasurer

A single businesswoman found she was terminally ill. She asked the doctor "Is there anything at all I can do?"

"Well," he mused, "You could try marrying a farmer.

"Will that help me live longer?"

"No. But it will certainly seem longer."

Fordyce Maxwell, formerly Scotsman

During the early days of the second World War, German aircraft came over to bomb the Clyde shipyards. In a small village to the south side of Glasgow, the local Home Guard, including a good few farmers were used to help the locals into air raid shelters. All was going well until one elderly lady came out of the shelter. "I'm going back to the house to get my teeth," she told the Home Guard man.

As he pushed her back into the shelter, he told her, "Listen it's bombs they are dropping. Not sausage rolls."

Hazel Howatson, Stone of Morphie

Some auction marts are famed for the food they provide. Others are not. One in the latter category saw the old farmer complain, "What kind of soup is this?" Only to be told, "It's bean soup." "I don't care what it has been. I want to know what it is now."

Anon

I spent my time as a mud student in Dumfriess-shire on a large upland unit which stretched to a hill hirsel where a herd of hill cows were kept. All were known to the shepherds and some had, over the years, acquired names such as 'The Bushes' because she had a habit of calving in the bushes. Another after the local vet who had treated her. A third one was called 'Doonican' which I took to be after Val Doonican the Irish singer. But, no, it was because every year when she calved she went "doon agin."

Robert Barr, Woodhouse

The following story was told about the late Tom Elliot while he was stewarding at the Highland Show. The judge had been taking his time sorting out the sheep classes.

During the judging of the ewe lamb class, Tom Elliot said, "Judge, if you dinnae hurry up with the ewe lambs they will be gimmers by the time you finish."

Allan Murray, Redden Farm

Two farming widowers were discussing their late wives, how much they missed them and how much thought they had put in to headstones. One had erected an ornate headstone with a long, flowery inscription. The other said: "I thought hard about it and eventually settled for 'Till Day Breaks.' It's short, beautiful – and cheap."

Fordyce Maxwell, formerly Scotsman

A Scottish farmer at Smithfield, in the days of telephone operators, is having trouble phoning his sister from a phone box. So he calls the operator who asks in a plummy voice, "Is there money in the box?"

"Naw, it's just me."

Iain McCrone, Cardsknolls

The vet drove as quickly as possible to see the cow down with staggers. Pulling up in the farmyard, he met a frantic Ben waving a rifle.

'She's dead,' he said. 'I'll need a certificate.'

The vet followed Ben into the field to check the cow.

'Ben, I need to certify the cow as fit for human consumption to write a certificate so you will get compensation from the BSE scheme. However, this cow clearly died from a gunshot,' he said looking at the hole in the cow's head.

'But vitnary, she's only going for toast'

(In Aberdeenshire they referred to the incinerator as going for toast)

Kate Richards, London

The late Charlie McCombie - whose son and namesake continues to farm at Auchincrieve, Huntly - was a useful and hard-tackling centre half for Huntly in the Highland League during the war and in the immediate post-war years when many foodstuffs, including eggs, were still rationed. At that time, a rumour got up that a scout from Aberdeen was coming out to see him play with a view to signing him for Aberdeen, then playing in the old Scottish First Division.

Sure enough, the scout arrived and Charlie played a "stormer" which he was confident would have impressed the scout, who came up to him afterwards and said: "You McCombie?" "Aye," said Charlie. "They tell me you're a fairmer," said the scout. "Aye," said Charlie. "Could you manage me a dizen eggs," the scout asked. And that was the last Charlie ever heard of him!

Eddie Gillanders, Farm North East

An enthusiastic Primary 7 schoolboy from Barrhill was asked by his teacher about the parable of the lost sheep. "Why was there such rejoicing in heaven when the lost sheep was found, making the flock back up to 100?"

Enthusiastically he offered the suggestion. "Was it because it was the tup, miss?"

John Scott, MSP

A farmer was walking in a field when he came across a lamp partially buried in the ground. He picked up the lamp and gave it a rub. A genie appeared and told him he had been granted one wish.

The man thought for a moment and said, "I want to live forever."

"Sorry," said the genie, "I'm not allowed to grant eternal life."

"OK, then, I want to die after the Government cuts taxes, balances the budget and eliminates the national debt."

"You crafty little beggar!" said the genie.

Dave Balfour, Auchtermuchty

Farm roups were often the scene of many a party. On the way home from a sale near Dunkeld, my colleague Jimmy Downie and I came across a drunk character crawling up the road on his hands and knees. He was well known to us as an agricultural rep who had clearly been partying at the sale.

We then discovered his car still running even although it was sitting on top of a hedge. We decided to take both him and his car back to his home. Jimmy bravely went to our hero's house and rang the bell. A lady opened the door and seemed somewhat surprised to see the drunk on her doorstep. However she took him in and we went home.

We discovered later that we had delivered our friend to his first wife who had divorced him some two years before.

David Leggat, United Auctions

David MacFarlane was a rep for Agrii. One day he paid a visit to a customer to drum up fertiliser sales. He found the farm close unusually quiet, save for an eager collie dog, which seemed to point the way through a door, as if the farmer was on the other side. David obliged by opening the door and followed through, only to be met by a volley of curses and variations on, "Who the h*ll are you?" The farmer and worker had just finished laying a large area of still wet concrete, which the collie was now prancing around on. He said he would come back some other time.

Peter Stewart, Urquhart

At the feein' market, a prospective farm employer spotted a strong looking loon. "Are ye seeking a fee?" "Aye sir." "Weel, it's thirty shillings the quarter plus your keep...ony questions?"

"Weel fairmer Ah hae a fair appetite and in the mornin' Ah aye start wi' twa or three plates o' parritch followed by half a dizzen biled eggs and aboot ten slice o' loaf a' washed doon wi' a gallon o' tea." "And fit aboot yer denner?" "Oh, afore ma denner, Ah need a mornin' fly...twa or three slice o' loaf wi' cheese and a gallon o' tea. And then at denner time, twa or three plates o' broth, maybe mince and tatties then rhubarb and custard. Ah'm richt fond o' rhubarb." "And for yer supper?" " Oh, afore ma supper, Ah'll need an efterneen fly...twa or three slice o' loaf wi' jam and mair tea. And then at supper, twa or three yalla fish fillets wi' half a dizzen poached eggs and mair loaf. And then if yer wife is a baker, some braw aipple sponge and custard." "Richt," said the farmer not impressed. "Ah dinna think Ah can fee ye, but if ye dae get fixed up, get in touch...Ah'll pay ye a guid price for yer dung!"

Ross Muir, Retired PR Limekilns

"I was standing on a beach on Tiree, a very low lying island, with a local farmer. We were discussing the danger of tsunamis or tidal waves in such a place. He said to me, "Aye Mr McGrigor, chest imagine if you and I are standing here and a bloody great satsuma is rolling towards us."

Jamie McGrigor MSP

The newly married farmer came in for dinner one day and found his wife in tears. Between sobs he found out that she had baked him a meat pie but that the cat had eaten it.

"That's no problem," he consoled her, "We can easily get another cat."

George Burgher, formerly Orkney & Shetland NFUS secretary

An elderly farming couple had just learned how to send text messages on their mobile phones. The wife was a romantic type and the husband was more of a no-nonsense guy.

One afternoon the wife went out to meet a friend for coffee.

She decided to send her husband a romantic text message and she wrote: "If you are sleeping, send me your dreams. If you are laughing, send me your smile. If you are eating, send me a bite. If you are drinking, send me a sip. If you are crying, send me your tears. I love you."

The husband texted back to her: "I'm on the toilet. Please advise."

Dave Balfour, Auchtermuchty

Visits to Frank Roger, Kenly Green, Boarhills were always interesting. When weed walking each spring in the 1960s I was required to compete with him to find the first tare. In the autumn, when soil sampling with the SAI rep, we were not left on our own as happened on other farms where we were just given a field map and left to walk over the designated fields.

No, this was usually an event which Frank Roger was out to enjoy. He drove us to different strategic points on the farm, giving the directions one of us should take, before racing off with the other to a distant part of the farm.

Later, he would chide us for being much slower than he would have been. This harangue made no allowance for us having to traverse by a V or in bigger fields, a W pattern when taking random samples rather than his much more simple diagonal line.

Sandy Millar, consultant formerly SAI

After starting his business in Balmullo, David Wilson did a job for a local farmer. When the work was finished the farmer said, "When you send in the account, I won't pay it, but when you need the money just come and ask for it."

On orders from his wife Mairi, who was responsible for the business accounts, David was sent to the farm to collect the money. The farmer's first words were "You'll be wanting some siller then." "Well, if you can spare it," replied David. "I canna spare it but you'd better come in," stated the old farmer. In his office, the drawer was overflowing with accounts, but he found the right one and David came home with a cheque, just as if it was a normal thing to do.

David Wilson, Balmullo

A series of comments met by one of the fairer sex who farms: "Presumably you mean a farmer's wife." A comment to me by the head mistress when I told her, aged 11, that I wanted to be a farmer.

--

"Why are you not married?" The first question I was asked by an elderly farmer who was supposed to mentor me.

"How am I supposed to know if the tup is working properly if I am not married?" This was my tongue in cheek response to him.

--

"Are you still farming?" Asked by friends who assumed my farming was no more than a passing phase.

--

"Is the farmer about?" This is a regular first question by a cold caller. I do not mind this as it gives me an excuse to avoid the caller.

--

"You had better see the boss. You have just walked past her." A comment by my tractor driver to a young salesman.

--

"You are not a real farmer, are you?" Comment from lady I met at a party.

--

"What the hell do you think you are doing?" said by me to a young couple who had parked their car in my farm road at the height of harvest. I realised as soon as I had said it, they knew what they were doing or wanting to do.

All from Mary Singleton, St Cyrus

A farmer's friend was fed up listening to him always moaning about how things were tough being a farmer. The weather was always wrong, the yield from the crops was always poor, feed prices were too high, the lambs weren't doing, the bull wasn't doing its work, cattle prices were on the floor etc. etc. He had heard it all ad infinitum.

One particular year it was well documented that it had been a bumper year for all types of farming, especially arable crops. The farmer's friend couldn't wait to point out that there was nothing he could moan about this year. The farmer had a long thoughtful pull on his pipe and said, "Aye, but what's it taken oot o the grund."

Michael Malone

Back in the 1950s when the Scottish Dairy Show was held in Glasgow, the overnight accommodation for the stockmen was a large dormitory. Similar to an army barracks, the beds were placed side by side the length of the building. Because of the sheer number of stockmen, the beds were close together and entry had to be gained by climbing in at the end. Soon the whole row of stockmen were side by side fast asleep. However, Jim Lawrie and a few other young blades brought a ewe and her two lambs – they were part of a livestock exhibition linked to the show – into the dormitory. The lads took the lambs to one end of the beds and the ewe to the other and then released the fretting mother. Leaving a trail of utter chaos in her wake after she spied her offspring, she charged down the dormitory over the sleeping bodies towards them.

George Lawrie, NFUS treasurer

TWO

A motorist stops in a layby. He notices two guys working. On further study he realises that one guy digs a hole then the other one fills it in. Puzzled, he went out to enquire further

"Ma name's Wullie an ah dig holes," says one.

"Ma names Tam an ah full in holes," says the other.

"What's the point?" asks the motorist.

Wullie replies, "We normally work as a three, Hughie pits in the trees but he's oan holiday this wik!"

Jim McColl, Beechgrove Garden

Three noted cattle breeders were having a drink and chat at a bull sale when the talk turned from cattle and farming to how to lose weight. They discussed various diets they had tried, from cabbage to F-Plan, agreeing that none had worked and how difficult it was to lose poundage. At which a stockman who had been listening while fitting in a quick drink before getting back to his bulls, said over his shoulder as he left: "Ony o' you lot ever thought o' work?"

Fordyce Maxwell, formerly Scotsman

The farmers at the market were discussing the move to change a local pub into a brothel when one of less knowledgeable in the gathering commented. "If they canna mak money selling beer, they hae nae chance selling soup."

Anon

The only cow in a small town in Ireland stopped giving milk. Then the town folk found they could buy a cow in Scotland quite cheaply. So, they brought the cow over from Scotland. It was absolutely wonderful. It produced lots of milk every day and everyone was happy. They bought a bull to mate with the cow to get more cows, so they'd never have to worry about their milk supply again. They put the bull in the pasture with the cow but whenever the bull tried to mount the cow, the cow would move away. No matter what approach the bull tried, the cow would move away from the bull, and he was never able to do the deed. The people were very upset and decided to go to the vet, who was very wise, tell him what was happening and ask his advice.

"Whenever the bull tries to mount our cow, she moves away. If he approaches from the back, she moves forward. When he approaches her from the front, she backs off. If he attempts it from the one side, she walks away to the other side."

The vet rubbed his chin thoughtfully and pondered this before asking, "Did you by chance, buy this cow in Scotland?"

The people were dumbfounded, since no one had ever mentioned that they had brought the cow over from Scotland.

"You are truly a wise vet," they said. "How did you know we got the cow from Scotland?

The vet replied with a distant look in his eye, "My wife is from Scotland."
Gilmour Lawrie, Queensland

Dougie was an hour late coming to the NFUS Council meeting. Grabbing a seat alongside colleagues on the Press table, he whispered, "What is he talking about?" as the European Commission guy droned on. "Not a clue," admitted Dougie's neighbour on the press bench.

"And I don't think he has either," chimed in another.
One of the agricultural press

The same Jimmy Nicol was primarily a beef farmer. Dairy farmers tended to be married as - to be politically incorrect about it - they needed a wife sometimes to milk the cows but certainly to separate the milk and the cream and make the butter and cheese. Although a bachelor, Jimmy made sure his staff received the "perks" which most farm workers received in those days, including milk and tatties. As he wasn't a dairy farmer, the milk had to be collected daily from the end of the road by the cattleman's wife. On this particular day, Jimmy came along in his Humber car (he was so small he could hardly see over the top of the steering wheel) to find the cattleman's wife at the end of the road, soaked to the skin, collecting the milk. She jumped in to the car, gave herself a shake to get the rain off her coat and castigated Jimmy: "Fit wye can ye nae get a wife and hae yer ane dairy?" she demanded.

"Uh," said Jimmy. "I'd get mair milk oot o' a coo!"
Eddie Gillanders, Farm North East

In the heyday of the Perth Bull Sales in the post WW2 era, it was traditional for breeders to visit herds prior to the sales to assess the opposition and to look out for new stock bulls. Sometimes they formed groups and included in their numbers exporters who had commissions to buy for overseas clients. Lavish hospitality would be accorded to such visiting parties.

And so it was at lunch a prominent breeder hosting such a delegation sat at one end of the table conducting conversation with his potential buyers and his rather austere wife sat in silence at the other. In an effort to break the ice, one of the visitors enquired if she took an interest in the herd.

"If it was not for my money there would be no cattle here," she replied.

Her husband, having overheard, broke off his conversation, looked up and commented, "No my dear and you would not be here either."
Donald Biggar, Chapelton

One Sunday morning the minister was disappointed to find that his congregation consisted of only one farmer. Wondering whether to he should hold the service, he decided to ask the farmer's opinion. "If I take a bag of feed to my sheep and only one turns up, I don't send it away hungry."

Moved by this simple analogy, the minister delivered a lengthy sermon. At the end of the service he asked the farmer if he had enjoyed it. "When only one ewe turns up, I don't give it the whole bag," was the response.

George Burgher, formerly Orkney & Shetland NFUS secretary

Someone asked the farmer if he had seen the film about the tractor. The farmer replied, "No, but I have seen the trailer."

Rosemary Walker, Playfair Walker PR

A lifelong town dweller, tired of the rat race, decided he was going to give up the town life, move to the country and become a chicken farmer. He bought a nice readymade chicken farm and moved in. As it turned out his next door neighbour was also a chicken farmer. The neighbour came for a visit one day and said, "Chicken farming isn't easy. Tell you what. To help you get started I'll give you 100 chickens."

The new farmer was thrilled. Two weeks later the neighbour dropped by to see how things were going. The new farmer said, "Not too well. All 100 chickens died." The neighbour said, "Oh I can't believe that. I've never had any trouble with my chickens. I'll give you 100 more." Another two weeks went by and the neighbour stopped by again. The new farmer said, "You're not going to believe this, but the second batch of chickens died too." Astounded the neighbour asked, "What went wrong?"

The new farmer said, "Well, I'm not sure whether I'm planting them too deep or too close together."

Iain McCrone, Cardsknolls

A Travel Agent looked up from his desk to see an old lady and an old farmer peering in the shop window at the posters showing the glamorous destinations around the world.

The agent had had a good week and the dejected couple looking in the window gave him a rare feeling of generosity.

He called them into his shop, "I know that on your pension it would probably be difficult for you to ever hope to have a real holiday, so I am sending you off to a fabulous resort at my expense. I won't take no for an answer."

He asked his secretary to write two flight tickets and to arrange for a room in a five star hotel.

As can be expected, the elderly pair accepted with gratitude, and were off.

About a month later the little old lady came in to his shop. "And how did you like your holiday?" he asked eagerly.

"The flight was exciting and the room was lovely," she said. "I've come to thank you, but one thing puzzled me. Who was that old b****r I had to share the room with?"

Dave Balfour, Auchtermuchty

The Lairg sale of North Country Cheviot lambs is the biggest one day sale in the country and a good draw was important. Although a public ballot was held to decide the order of sale, there were rumblings of discontent about who would draw the ballot. United Auctions decided to invite the local Free Church minister to officiate and draw the ballot. He, along with a minister called Mr McLean from the neighbouring parish, were both regular sellers from their Glebe. Out of 32,000 lambs on sale that day, Mr McLean was pulled out as second last consignor. His consignments of five ewe lambs included one which was black. Following the auctioneer's reference to the parable and despite the lateness of the day, the consignment achieved one of the top prices of the day. The trade was also chased on by faithful parishioners from his other flock!

David Leggat, United Auctions

One of the big problems for compound feed manufacturers has been getting the firmness of the cake just right. Too firm and the animal does not get the full benefit of the cake. Too slack and it just goes into a mush in the bag. As a feed salesman, I used to occasionally receive complaints. On one farm where the complaint had been made, the pellets were too firm, I was shown a sample pellet. Gingerly I bit into it and said I did not think there was much wrong with it. It seemed just about right, I told the farmer. "No wonder," he said, "It has already been through the cow."

Anon

A mean farmer and his wife walked past a swanky new restaurant.

"Did you smell that food?" she asked. "Incredible."

Being a kind-hearted Scotsman, he thought, "What the heck. I'll treat her."

So, they walked past the restaurant again.

Colin Blair, Darwin

Rog Wood, Auchentaggart, could not understand why sheep in the Chernobyl affected area had to be checked for radio activity while farmers and shepherds who worked with the sheep did not. He was duly tested and thankfully confirmed he was not suffering from the caesium.

Rog Wood, Herald

This story is from my very first job in Devon. As a trainee accompanying my boss on a farm visit, we were invited into the kitchen for coffee. While our host took his boots off outside the back door, a cat that had been sleeping curled up on the window sill stood up and slowly walked away – to reveal underneath it a fruit cake. Presumably it was fresh from the Aga earlier that morning and it had been warming its backside nicely! The farmer walked in and kindly offered us not only a cup of coffee but a slice of fresh cake, which we politely declined!"

David Barnes, Chief Agricultural Officer SRPID

Picture the scene – family lunch, great uncle George sitting opposite four year old Elizabeth his great grandniece. They have never met before. As the meal progresses, George realises that Elizabeth has never taken her eyes off him. She hasn't eaten a bite. He becomes uneasy, embarrassed even. Eventually he asks her why she is staring at him so intently. The reply, "I'm waiting to see how you drink like a fish!"

Jim McColl, Beechgrove Garden

A shepherd who lived in the Merse,
Tried writing hilarious verse,
He wrote letter by letter
In the hope he got better,
Instead he got steadily poorer.

Bob Noble, formerly Duns and ex Borders NFU

The electrician's shop in Newburgh had a visit from a salesman from one of the companies that supply electric cables. A local farmer came in and started ranting about the poor quality of cable. The electrician stood back as the salesman extolled the excellence of his supplies. The farmer listened but was not giving up easily. "It may be ok for electricity but it is no use for towing tractors" and then he stomped out.

Maureen Burgess, Newburgh

During the war my father had gone out as usual to milk the cows at 3.30 am when he noticed parachutes falling all around the farm. Soldiers speaking a foreign language were invading the country side and running through the steading. Dad went back into the house to announce to Mum "The war is over, the Germans have landed".

When Mum asked what he was going to do he replied, "Get on with the milking, that can't wait."

It turned out the Free Polish Army, based in nearby Kinross were practising for future parachute drops into Europe.

Gilmour Lawrie, Queensland

Gavin Catto, College advisor for many years, gave a talk in Laurencekirk in the nineteen sixties and told the following story.

A farmer visited his neighbour for dinner one night and as was customary in the farming community after the meal, they went out and had a look at the cattle in the steading. On their way round the visitor said to his host, "John I am going to pay you a compliment." This was, and still is, a very unusual occurrence in farming circles but there was a sting in the tail. "You have the biggest rats here I have ever seen."

George Anderson, Mains of Kair

One of the features of the livestock auction rings, occurs when the auctioneer gets some last minute guidance from the seller. Most of this information is along the lines of "He is the best bull I have ever bred" or "She comes by" and then mentions a famous sire"

However when my young Charolais bull came into the ring, I announced to auctioneer David Leggat and to the throng around the ringside, "This young bull is so good on his feet, he could serve a nervous heifer on black ice."

Andrew Hornall, Falleninch

Perth Area NFU meetings were held in the lounge of the Birnam Hotel and the members sank out of sight in the deep lounge chairs. The press were stationed at the back of the room where we could only see the backs of the members' heads. The only way we could tell who was speaking was if their heads were moving.

Andrew Arbuckle

Mary Carbury was a Women's Land Army girl from Glasgow stationed on a farm on Arran. One day, the farmer said he was going over to the mainland and she was to stay and look after his cows. She saw them settled down at night but the next morning, they were gone. She went to the neighbouring farmer who denied all knowledge of the missing cattle but she soon identified them in one of his fields.

He claimed they must have strayed into his field by mistake. "And I suppose, they then milked themselves," replied this sharp as a pin Glaswegian.

Ann Young, Stirling

A chicken farmer was unhappy with the performance of his cockerel. He seemed to show no interest in the hens at all so he consulted with his vet to see if there was anything that could be done to help.

The vet said he had this product called Rooster Booster but he advised the farmer to be sparing with it and only to add a few drops of the potion to the cockerel's feed.

The farmer was leaving nothing to chance so he soaked the cockerel's next feed overnight in a tablespoon measure of Rooster Booster.

After his morning feed the cockerel started chasing the hens all over the yard - feathers were flying. In fact the cockerel also started chasing the ducks, the sheep and the goats such was the heightened level of his libido. By evening time the cockerel was gasping for breath, his eyes were wide open and bloodshot and the sweat was dripping off the end of his beak.

That evening when the farmer went to bed he said to his wife that he feared the cockerel would be dead in the morning if he didn't calm down.

Sure enough when the farmer parted the curtains in the morning and looked out, he could see the cockerel was lying with its heels up in the middle of the yard and the buzzards were circling overhead.

The farmer rushed down stairs and went out to retrieve the carcass but when he bent down to pick up the cockerel, the bird opened one eye and whispered, "Let them land".

Neale McQuistin, Airyolland

THREE

A Buchan fairmer had been into the mart in Aberdeen and got on the train to ging hame tae Maud. The train was busy and he struggled to find a seat.

Eventually, after checking lots of carriages, he found an empty seat wi a top hat sitting on it. He lifted the hat and sat doon. Five minutes later a posh gentleman appeared and said, "Excuse me my man but you're sitting in my seat. Didn't you see that I had my hat on it?"

The fairmer just looked at him and said, "In Buchan, it's airses that coont!"

Peter Chapman, Strichen

A farm shoot and Jock's Labrador Jip was on its first outing. At the first drive Jip took off and despite Jock's whistles, pleas and shouts, the dog caused havoc, scattering birds in every direction. An embarrassed and exasperated Jock started roaring "Jip ya hoor ye! Jip ya hoor ye!"

A rather posh lady gun from the Home Counties turned to Jock and enquired, "I say there my man, does your dog have a Gaelic name?"

Ross Muir, Retired PR, Limekilns

Two cows were taken to visit a neighbour's bull. They observed him pawing and pacing around at the other end of the paddock.

"I hope he doesn't charge us," said one cow to the other.

"I hope not as well," replied the other. "I haven't any money."

Sandy Scott, Dolphinston

Farmer, Sandy Thomson decided in retirement he wanted to go and see the Great Plains in the USA. Unfortunately his hard of hearing wife, Muggie, wanted to go too.

Later, cruising through Texas, he realised his rented car needed fuel and drew into a country petrol station.

A guy came out to serve him.

"Could I have some petrol please?" asked Sandy

"You mean gas," replied the attendant.

"Fit's 'at, fit's 'at, fit's he saying?" screeched Muggie.

Sandy; explained, "He says they call petrol gas here."

"Oh, oh, funny that," thought Muggie.

"If I open the bonnet will you top up the screenwash?" asked Sandy

"You mean the hood. We call the bonnet the hood," said the attendant.

Muggie again asked, "Fit's 'at, fit's 'at?"

Again Sandy explained, "He says they ca' the bonnet the hood here."

"Oh, oh, funny that," thought Maggie.

"I'll give your fenders a wipe down," said the attendant.

"The fenders?" queried Sandy.

"That's what you'd call the bumpers," replied the attendant.

"Fit's 'at, fit's 'at?" screeched Muggie

Sandy explained yet again, "He says they ca' bumpers fenders here."

Eventually the attendant recognised the Scottish accent and asked where they were from?

"Oh, just beside Aberdeen," said Sandy

"What a coincidence" said the attendant. "When I was a young man, I worked in the oil industry in Aberdeen just as it was kicking off. I stayed a few years and fell for a lovely young local girl but after we were married she turned into a complete witch so I upped and left."

"Fit's 'at, fits 'at, fit's he sayin?" screeched Muggie

Sandy replied, "He says he ken's yi."

Peter Cook, farm consultant

A North-east farmer and his orra loon are gathering in the last few sheaves of a successful harvest. The trailer is packed with a heavy load. They make it to the gate and without checking for passing traffic, take their place on the road and turn towards the farm. Unbeknown to them a new Porsche is being driven along the road at excessive speed. Suddenly the driver is faced with a tractor pulling a cart load of grain. With no alternative and in panic he is forced into the field from which the farmer and the orra loon have come.

The Porsche hurtles round the field twice, before crashing into the fence and being thrown into a ditch. The car is severely damaged, the driver shaken to bits.

The farmer looks back at the carnage, slightly bemused. "Gosh Jock did ye see that. We just got out of there in the nick of time."

Bill Howatson, formerly Press & Journal

The old shepherd was asked to judge a beauty contest at the local dance with the final line up to take place at 12 midnight. During the evening he slipped a 'finalist card' to his choice of six young ladies.

When the appointed hour arrived the six finalists went on parade. But it was obvious beauty was not their special attribute.

Asked afterwards what took him to select such a line up he remarked, "I've been a shepherd all my life, and if a ewe has not got six good front teeth and a good udder she is nae use to me. That is the way I judged them tonight."

Sandy Scott, Dolphinston

A college adviser known to be a difficult man to work with got a new job. He came out of the director's office after giving him the news and remarked to a colleague who had worked with him for several years, "The director says I'll leave a large hole."

His colleague barely looked up, "I fear you may have misheard him."

Fordyce Maxwell, formerly Scotsman

This tale concerns a trip I and three others, then young farmers, took to see Rangers versus Dundee United in a Scottish Cup final at Hampden Park. Only one of us had been to Hampden before. That was the driver so it should have been easy. The plan was to just follow the multitude of cars, vans, buses with scarves and mascots going along the carriageway. They all mysteriously disappeared at a junction, whilst we merrily flew along at speed only noticing, too late, that we were all alone and hopelessly lost.

After a few more wrong manoeuvres we ended up on the Great Western Road where we decided to seek help.

The car stopped and I jumped out, crossed the road and found a man who was leaning on a bus stop outside a pub. "Excuse me" I asked, "but can you tell me the way to Hampden?"

"Aye, nae bother," he replied, "in fact I'm going there myself." So without much more ado I jumped into the back of the car and our new guide jumped into the front.

"Now boys, I don't know the right road to Hampden 'cause I only know the bus routes." So we went the bus routes to Hampden.

As well as being a Rangers supporter, it also emerged that he was a boiler-maker on the Clyde and that he hailed from Drumchapel which he told us was on the north side of the river. As we travelled along he pointed out places of interest. After crossing the river Clyde, he asked, "Where are you boys fae anyway?"

I replied, "We're from near Peebles."

"Peebles? Peebles? What side of the water is that on?"

Robert Barr, Woodhouse

A farming couple were touring Scotland and staying in a Bed and Breakfast in Aberdeenshire. For breakfast each morning there was a very small container of honey on the table which would barely cover half a slice of toast. After a morning or two the annoyed visitors, holding up the small pot of honey said to their host, "We see that you must keep a bee."

George Anderson, Mains of Kair

A grandson was visiting his granda in the wee croft just north of Huntly where he had spent his whole working life. The youngster said "My dad says that you have a brother but that you have never seen him for fifty years. Is that richt granda?"

The auld man replied, "Aye thats richt. I hinnae seen him since he gid awa sooth fifty eer ago."

"Fifty eer is an awfa lang time granda he must hiv geen awfa far awa. Faur is he onywye?"

"Oh Aye he gid hyn awa tae Laurencekirk."

Peter Chapman, Strichen

The Dumfriesshire landowner had two daughters, one who married quickly and settled down, the younger less lucky in courtship. Distraught, she turns to her wealthy father and asks if he could arrange a grand ball in the village, invite all and sundry and see if she could meet a suitable man. The hairst had been good and the old man, mindful of his younger daughter's predicament, agreed. A grand ball was held, but at the end of the night the younger daughter was no further forward and over the ensuring months sank into deep melancholy.

Three years past and she asked her father if he could arrange another ball. The old man agreed and it was duly held, but with no luck for the lass. Another three years passed and again the younger daughter plucked up courage to ask the old man. The hairst had not been so good the last few years and the old man responded, "Lass, if you can't get a man with two balls, you'll not get one with three!"

Bill Howatson, formerly Press & Journal

One long time livestock exhibitor was once asked why he was no longer showing his sheep. He stroked his chin and replied, "All my judges are now dead and there is no point."

Anon

A well-known farmer was stressed out after a busy lambing season.

His wife insisted he went to the doctor and eventually she took him. In the surgery the doctor gave him a thorough check over.

"You're badly stressed. I don't think I've ever seen a case quite like it. Could I have a word with your wife while you wait in the car?"

So the wife went in to hear the diagnosis.

"Mrs Smith, it's the worst case of stress I've ever seen. Unless he gets proper treatment, he's going to die."

"Is there anything I can do doctor?"

"Tender loving care could be the answer. What would be good for him would be for him to wake up to a nice mug of tea and a slice of lightly buttered toast. While he's enjoying that you could run him a warm bath.

While he's in the bath you could prepare him a nice breakfast of scrambled egg with smoked salmon and a glass of bucks fizz just to get the day going.

"I think for lunch, some asparagus with melted butter and a glass of Sauvignon Blanc and for supper a nice piece of fillet steak done medium rare along with two or three glasses of good claret. Finally just before bedtime, a big chunk of mature stilton."

When she got back to the car her husband asked her, "Well what did the doctor say?"

"He said you're going to die................

Arthur Anderson, formerly BBC Landward producer

Two old farmers were being entertained watching a cockerel chasing a hen round a stack of oat sheaves. They farmers were chuckling, as every time the pair went round the cockerel seemed to be catching up on the hen. Just at that an ear of corn fell onto the ground from the top of the stack and the next time around the cockerel stops and pecks at the ear of corn.

Observing this, one of the farmers said to the other, "I hope I never get to be that hungry."

Neale McQuistin Airyolland

On Islay, the sale was held up as one of the main buyers, Willie Low, a cattle dealer from Aberdeen had been delayed by the late sailing of the ferry over to Islay. Eventually the taxi turned up. Low was offered a cup of tea or a whisky. "Now, now you know it is far too early in the day to have a cup of tea," he responded.

Jim Dunn, Retired Auctioneer, Tillicoultry

The first chairman of the now defunct Buchan Meat when chairing a members meeting had as a guest speaker, a solicitor who spoke for two and a half hours solid. To make matters worse, his speech was exceptionally dry.

Later the solicitor asks how he thought his talk went down. "Well," he said, "You fairly shortened the winter."

Peter Cook, farm consultant

An Orkney young crofter had courted a neighbouring farmer's daughter for several years and eventually picked up enough courage to ask her father if he could marry her.

"A'll think aboot hid," was the reply.

"Can you support a family?"

"I cheust want Maggie," exclaimed the crofter.

George Burgher, formerly Orkney & Shetland NFUS secretary

During the BSE crisis, two cows were having a conversation and one said to the other, "Aren't you worried about this mad cow disease?"

The other replied, "Why should I? I'm a duck."

Rosemary Walker, Playfair Walker PR

When the "new" mart was built out the Crieff Road in Perth none were happier than the motley but skilled, crew of photographers who had previously endured major problems finding a quiet spot to photograph the champion bulls down at the old Caledonian Road mart.

There every time, we, photographers had found a quiet corner, some bright spark parked a car or trailer or dumped a load of neeps or straw bales in our space. No matter what complaints we made to the management to reserve a place, it just never lasted and made the job of the cameramen more difficult and frustrating than it need have been.

Although we were familiar with every corner of the premises and loved the old place it came as a great opportunity to find a place of our own when the new market was built.

The management was amenable to this and we agreed on a spot, an outside wall at the west end of the buildings and we were told to choose what colour we would favour for our new Studio background – joy unbounded.

The arrangement worked pretty well during the first day`s judging but when the sale started the next day an unexpected problem arose when the sold animals were being loaded onto the lorries which were parked in the same area; the movement of men, beasts and lorries caused too much distraction for the animals being photographed and made many of them jumpy and fractious.

This led to a good deal of wasted time as the stockmen patiently moved this foot and that foot, then had to walk their charges round in an attempt to settle them.

It came to a head when, late in the day, as the light was fading and cattle, stockmen and photographers were becoming increasingly tired and impatient. The top priced bull of the sale had to be photographed for the next day`s newspapers. Before digital cameras and computers, time for processing the films was an important factor in making the deadlines and as the time wore on the tension rose.

The champion was shunted this way and that to suit the photographers` needs and of course conflicting opinions on what was right started to boil up.

"Up a bit on the front feet."

"Naw that's ower much."

" We're needin' that far awa hint leg forrit."

"Naw ye've got him stretched noo."

"Get the lugs up."

This went on for about 20 minutes and the tension built to anger. The atmosphere became electric and fisticuffs amongst the photographers became increasingly likely.

"Go on jist walk him roon' one mair time".

The stockman, firmly holding the halter and breathing heavily, went to oblige but the beast backed up onto our new painted sea-green studio wall and lifted his tail bringing an anguished scream from one of the tortured camera men.

"Dinna let him sh*te on the wa."

This broke the tension all round and resulted in the photographers and spectators doubled up laughing and even rolling on the ground. I don't think the bewildered stockman even smiled but we all became pals again.

Louis Flood, Photographer

An Irishman came over to Scotland for the 'tattie howking' but after a couple of dreich wet weeks he thought there must be an easier way to make a living. As a first step he decided that learning to speak the Queen's English as it is spoken would make a big difference. He thought the best way to do this was to shut himself in a dark room with a wet towel over his head and after a week he felt he was good enough to test progress in real life. He walked into a shop, shoulders back and head high, and said in his best accent, "Good morning my man could I have a packet of Panatellas, a box of Swan Vestas and a Courier please?"

The reply was, "Are you Irish?"

"To be sure but how did you know that?" he asked.

"Because this is a butcher's shop," was the response.

Alistair Donaldson, formerly Meat and Livestock Commission

A young and slightly built lady vet, not long into her first employment, quickly realised that, for any of the heavier jobs, farmer clients much preferred one of her male colleagues.

One afternoon, when all the other vets were out on call and she was alone in the surgery, the phone rang. A farmer needed a vet urgently to calve a cow.

When she arrived the farmer and two men in boiler suits were waiting. Seeing her, the farmer's face fell. Pretending not to notice and wanting to appear efficient and business-like, she told one of the men to steady the cow's head. After roping the calf's legs and positioning the jack she told the other to crank it when she said.

Eventually the calf was born and soon had its head up. "Well then," she said, "that went fine." Just then one of the men bolted round the corner of a building and was very audibly sick. "Yes," the farmer replied "but I did think you were a wee bit hard on those two fellows from Scottish Power."

P.S. The young lady vet is now Lord (or should it be Lady) Lieutenant of Berwickshire

John Elliot Roxburgh Mains

Gorgie market in Edinburgh is no more but in its heyday in mid 1990s, the Tuesday prime sale day saw many good bullocks topping £1000, for the first time ever.

On one such day, after his stint in the rostrum, Kenny Robertson headed to the mart restaurant for a well-earned lunch, where he joined a group of farmers having their coffee and cakes.

No sooner had he sat down, than they tackled him. "They big bullocks o' oors, ye're chairging us far ower much commission."

He responded, "You realise that you're all sitting here, scoffing cakes and buns with your sales cheques already in your pockets. How long do you wait for your grain cheques?"

"That's as may be. Onywye, we're telling ye that yer commissions far ower high."

"Tell you what, you're all highly valued customers and I don't want to lose you so you must keep this strictly to yourselves and not a word to anyone else. Is that agreed?"

"Agreed"

"Right. Seeing you have promised to keep quiet, from now on, I personally promise that you will be charged 3% commission on your fat cattle from next Tuesday but mind, not a word to another soul or the deal's off."

"That's just great isn't it lads? Ah telt ye that he would see us aright. We jist hud tae ask him."

Old Jim had been sitting quietly in the corner, observing but saying nothing. "Jim, yer no saying ower much but 3% commission, is that no just grand?"

The old worthy replied, "Ye great bunch o' stipid b⁺ggers. He's caught ye all oot. We're only paying two and three quarter % at the meenit. Ye've just agreed to 3%."

Stony silence ensued as the auctioneer picked up his well-earned lunch and moved to another table where he received a quiet wink and sly grin from old Jim.

Kenny Robertson, Robertson Rural

A farmer emailed his neighbour and said, "I feel very bad about it but I must confess to you that I have been using your wife a lot recently when you were away especially at weekends and I am so sorry about it. Alan."

His neighbour was furious, got his gun and shot his wife. When he returned to his computer there was another email from Alan saying, "I just noticed in the email I sent you my auto correct had changed wifi to wife and I didn't notice it before I sent it. I now have my own wifi fixed. Alan."

Jack Lawson, Cattle Improvement Service

The store sales held every autumn on the Western Islands were notorious for the amount of whisky consumed. One year on Islay at Tom Epps' draft sale of cattle a big number of buyers from mainland were over. They included John Oswald who used to graze hundreds of island cattle. He and his pal, Tom Graham found a table to sit at as the sale went on and Mrs Epps gave them bottle of whisky. The sale was a flyer but Oswald hardly had a bid in. By the time the sale finished so was the whisky. "Mrs Epps more whisky please," he asked. She responded "Next time you come bring your own whisky." He retorted, "Next time, I will bring my own cattle."

Jim Dunn, Retired auctioneer, Tillicoultry

An Aussie farmer walks into an outback cafe with a full-grown emu behind him.

The waitress asks them for their orders.

The Farmer says, "A hamburger, chips and a coke," and turns to the emu, "What's yours?"

"Sounds great, I'll have the same," says the emu.

A short time later the waitress returns with the order. "That will be $9.40 please," and he reaches into his pocket and pulls out the exact change and pays.

The next day, the man and the emu come again and he says, "A hamburger, chips and a coke."

The emu says, "Sounds great, I'll have the same."

Again the farmer reaches into his pocket and pays with exact change.

This becomes routine until the two enter again. "The usual?" asks the waitress.

"No, it's Friday night, so I'll have a steak, baked potato and a salad," says the man.

"Same for me," says the emu.

Shortly the waitress brings the order and says, "That will be $32.62."

Once again the man pulls the exact change out of his pocket and places it on the table.

The waitress cannot hold back her curiosity any longer. "Excuse me

mate, how do you manage to always pull the exact change from your pocket every time?"

"Well, love," says the farmer, 'a few years ago, I was cleaning out the back shed and found an old lamp. When I cleaned it, a genie appeared and offered me two wishes.

"My first wish was that if I ever had to pay for anything, I would just put my hand in my pocket and the right amount of money would always be there."

"That's brilliant," says the waitress. "Most people would ask for a million dollars or something, but you'll always be as rich as you want, for as long as you live."

"That's right. Whether it's a gallon of milk or a Rolls Royce, the exact money is always there," says the man..

Still curious the waitress asks, "What's with the bloody emu?"

"Well my second wish was for a tall bird with a big a**e and long legs and who agrees with everything I say."

Gilmour Lawrie, Queensland

FOUR

The late Maitland Mackie, who was always ready to make a self-deprecating joke against himself, once wandered down to the harvest field and told his combine driver to go away home for lunch and he would finish off the field. Maitland duly finished the field and moved in to the next-door field. Shortly afterwards, his neighbour, the former Highland Show chairman, Jack Sleigh, pulled up and got out of his car. "Foo are ye gettin' on, Maitland, foo's it rinnin'?" he asked. "Oh," said Maitland. "It's a grand crop - must be about four tonnes to the acre." "Well," said Jack. "I'm afa' pleased aboot that 'cos it's my field!"

Eddie Gillanders, Farm North East

John Hay of Carlungie, Carnoustie was a member of the now disbanded Potato Marketing Board. At Angus NFU Area meetings, fellow potato growers eagerly awaited his feedback. During the period when the future of the Board came under judicial review, Hay's reports reached orations of Churchillian magnificence and some believed tickets could have been sold for the meetings.

Not everyone appreciated so much potato talk however. One evening, dairy farmer, Gordon Law from Glentyrie, at Redford exploded after sitting through a PMB report, an NFUS potato committee report and a Scottish Seed Potato Development Council report. "It's nothing but tatties at these meetings," he complained. "How about something else for a change?"

His cry, although well warranted, went largely unheeded.

Ewan Pate, Courier

The loon was sent to the big city to collect some cattle the farmer had bought. Unused to city ways, he parked his tractor and trailer on double yellow lines outside the mart. On his return he saw one of the Yellow Peril brigade fixing a penalty notice to the windscreen of the tractor.

"What is that for?" asked the loon, "The sign says 'Fine for Parking'."

Anon

A rather dim Aberdeenshire farm loon was instructed to take a load of turnips to London. Never having been south of Stonehaven, his knowledge of "southern" towns and cities was somewhat limited. On reaching Edinburgh, he enquired of a passer-by: "Wid this be London by ony chance?" He was told he still had around 400 miles to go. He drove down the A1 and on reaching Newcastle made the same enquiry, same again in York and in Peterborough. Eventually he reached London in the middle of the night.

Driving around, he eventually spotted a likely looking lad. "Wid this be London by ony chance?" "Sure gov, this is London alright." Relief all round and then...."Far are ye needing yer neeps cowped?"

Ross Muir, Retired PR Limekilns

A newly qualified vet appeared on the farm to carry out some AI. His plummy voice did not go down well with the old farmer who asked if he was qualified.

"Oh yes, I passed all my exams and graduated last month," came the reply.

"In that case, the cows are in there," said the farmer who then left the vet to get on with the job.

The posh vet emerged from the shed an hour later and the farmer enquired as to how he got on.

"Oh top hole," came the plummy voiced reply.

"Ah bl**dy well thought so," retorted the farmer. "I knew you'd make an a**e of it."

Peter Small, Falfield

There was a food van at the farm roup and the sign advertising it said "Enjoy a pie and a friendly word."

Encouraged by this, I went up and asked for a pie, then asked the vendor "What about the friendly word?"

Back came the response, "Don't eat the pie."

James Black, Backboath

A semi retired farmer had been busy in the sheep pens all day. It had been very warm and by tea time he was really tired. When he sat down to tea he said this to his wife and told her he was going to bed early. She said, "Good idea, I'll have an early night too."

They got settled down, he on his right side and she at his back . "Oh," he thought, "I'm so tired if I could just get to sleep." He got a tap on the shoulder so turned to face his wife.

She said, "Do you remember when we were first married and when we went to bed you would hold my hand?" So he turned round and held her hand for a wee while, then got back onto his right side again and thought, "Oh I wish I could get to sleep. I'm so tired."

A wee while later came another tap on the shoulder, "Do you remember when we were first married and went to bed you would give me a big cuddle?"

So he put his arms round her and gave her a cuddle then got back on his right side and thought, "I'm so tired I wish I could get to sleep."

Following a third tap on the shoulder, he turned to face her. "Do you remember when we were first married and we went to bed, you would nibble my neck and give me love bites?"

With that he threw the duvet back and swung his legs over the side of the bed.

"Where do you think you're going?" she asked.

"I'm going to the bathroom to get my teeth."

Ronnie McLauchlan, Tulliemet

A farmer killed a deer and took it home to cook for dinner.

Both he and his wife decided that they wouldn't tell the kids what kind of meat it was, but would give them a clue and let them guess.

The kids were eager to know what the meat was on their plates, so they begged their dad the farmer for the clue.

Well, he said, 'It's what mummy calls me sometimes.'

The little girl screamed to her brother, "Don't eat it, it's an ar****le'

Dave Balfour, Auchtermuchty

United Auctions was one of a number of companies which ran auction marts in Glasgow.

Cattle and sheep occasionally escaped, much to the angst of the local population. After one such escape, a very irate lady stormed into the office and confronted the cashier on a sale day where she shouted at the top of her voice, "A bull has run up oor close and oor Jeanie's pregnant."

The cashier advised her to supply a vet's certificate and compensation would be considered the next week.

David Leggat, United Auctions

At a Young Farmers stock judging competition in Fife they were judging beef cattle and as usual had to assess them and then place A,B,X or Y in the right order.

One young farmer, after looking and feeling the bullocks on display, decided to mark them X first then B, Y and A.

X was probably the most out of breed character amid the four and the expert team of judges obviously wanted to know the reasons behind his decision.

After a shaky and very nervous start, with many references to his notes, he stated that the paramount reason that he considered X the winner was that he had by far the largest mouth and could therefore out eat the others and get to the market quicker!

Colin Blair, Darwin

Jock liked a good argument, especially with one of the local livestock dealers who supplied him with stallions and bulls. In the banter between them he never called the dealer a b*stard but always referred to him as a "poor faitherless boy".

George Burgher, formerly Orkney & Shetland NFUS secretary

Speaking at a dinner in Wooler a few years ago and at least 10 years before his farm was actually sold, Jim Stobo, Fishwick, expressed his concerns over unsubstantiated rumours that flew around the farming world. "Only last week I was disappointed to learn that Fishwick had been sold."

Then, he added, "I was even more disappointed to find out how little it had made."

Fordyce Maxwell, formerly Scotsman

On one occasion the wages inspector arrived to check all staff wages. He said Joe was underpaid in the winter but overpaid in the summer. He told me I would need to adjust this. I couldn't convince him that this made little sense so he insisted on seeing Joe. On arriving at the steading, Joe's opening remark was, "What are you needing?"

"I have come to talk to you about your wages," said the inspector.

"Well you can f**k off," said Joe. "That's between me and the fermer and f**k all to do with you, so f**k off out of my steading."

The inspector shook his head in dismay and beat a hasty retreat.

Willie Porter, West Scryne

Horse sales are in a class of their own for producing characters and stories.

A young auctioneer was struggling to sell a horse for a titled lady. As the bidding came to a close the lady was hesitant to take the price and expressed her disappointment. She then asked if the horse was destined for dressage. The auctioneer replied, "Sadly not, my lady, more like sausage!"

David Leggat, United Auctions

Back in the late 1990s a group of Scottish growers and scientists visited Finland to study the health benefits of eating lots of soft fruit. For some reason we ended up in the remote forest town of Ilomantsi right up against the Russian border. Its main claim to fame is that it is the most easterly town in the European Union (about the same longitude as Cairo, since you ask.) Otherwise its only distinguishing feature is a very tall structure that had been a water tower which had been converted into a restaurant. It was like a giant toadstool with a very long stem and a mushroom shaped top which had housed the water tank. The Russians didn't like it because it was on the top of a small hill and afforded a fantastic view deep into their territory. Anyway, to mark our visit, the civic leaders of Ilomantsi asked us to an evening reception in this elevated restaurant. When our party of around a dozen arrived at the base, we discovered that the lift only held around three people and was extremely slow. It had probably been designed just to take workmen up to inspect the tank. I spotted a stairwell and rather than wait I decided to lead an expedition up this alternative route. A handful of us set out but it was a hard climb with about 200 steps and no landings to stop to regain our breath. It was stamina sapping work but it was simply a case of onwards and upwards. Completely out of breath I eventually reached a heavy steel door and as I opened it I turned to the guy behind me and said "I'm b*ggered!"

Just with that, a man with the mayor's gold chain round his neck stepped eagerly forward from behind the door and grabbed my hand . "Hello B*ggared," he said, "Welcome. I am Timo, the mayor of Ilomantsi." He then spent the whole evening using my new name!

Ewan Pate, Courier

This story is told of Tom Barr, legendary farmer from Knocktim, Kirkcolm.

Years ago, he 'phoned up his bank manager. "Can ye come roon?"

"Certainly Mr Barr. To what do I owe this kind invitation?"

"I want to show you the new combine you've just bought me," replied Tom.

Alec Ross, Stranraer

On a wet and stormy day the farmer was issuing the days instructions to his staff.

"This is no day for the horses to be out so will those of you who have coats and leggings go and scale hotts." (Hotts being the clumps of dung laid out in heaps in fields ready to be spread by hand as fertiliser.)

After a suitable pause he continued, "and those who have no coats or leggings just go along with them."

Donald Biggar, Chapelton

You can lead a cow upstairs but not down. It's the way their joints don't oppose. One poor farmer found out the hard way.

"Come on, Daisy, down you go."

"I can't go downstairs, it's the way my joints are."

"I don't care about your joints. The wife's coming home in five minutes. Get down the stairs."

Gerry Watson, Perth and Garador

Echoing the difficulty farmers have in dealing with supermarkets, the following question and answer occurred at the Oxford Farming Conference one year.

"What is the difference between supermarkets and terrorists?"

The farmers' answer, "You can negotiate with terrorists."

David Cranstoun, retired SAC advisor

The story is told that Lord Forteviot, who was a well-known breeder of Aberdeen-Angus at Dupplin, in his capacity as chairman of Dewar's whisky went to a funeral with the boss of Bell's whisky. They stopped for lunch and the Bell's man offered his Lordship a drink. "I suppose you'll want one of your own," he said to Lord Forteviot. "No, no," the noble Lord replied. "I'll just have one of yours. I wouldn't like to go to a funeral smelling of drink!"

Eddie Gillanders, Farm North East

A farmer had a sign at gate into field. 'Please, when entering make sure you can run across the field in nine seconds.'

When asked why, he replied, "The bull can do it in ten."

Gavin Hill, SAC Consulting

A Highlander met a fellow crofter and told him that he had bought a goat. "I haven't seen it around." To which the crofter responded that it was rather small and weakly so he was keeping it under the bed meantime. "What about the smell?" "It doesn't seem to mind the smell", was the reply.

George Burgher, formerly Orkney & Shetland NFUS secretary

At a distant "Whisky Olympics" show at Dalmally, Fletch (Kenny Fletcher, Scottish Farmer) and I bumped into Ewan MacPherson, Millhouse, Barcaldine by Oban.

"Boys," quoth he, with his big smile, "It looks like rain. We'd better take shelter". This was MacPherson speak for "we are going for a dram."

Mind you, had the weather been sunshine the same shelter would have been sought for refuge from the heat. There was no way out.

En route to "the tent," with some enthusiastic followers, Ewan suggested I go find his best sidekick Dochy Buchanan, Shenavallie, Oban and fetch him to the refreshment placie.

I eventually found Dochy round the sheep pens and passed on the invite from Ewan. "I can't, John," he said, reaching into his jacket pocket and bringing out a small bottle, "I'm on pills for my vagina."

This rather startling news took me aback a bit, but Dochy ploughed blithely on "and it says on the bottle No Alcohol."

"Well, Ewan's expecting you anyway, Dochy," says I. So we made our way to the most popular tent on the showground where the drams had already been set up.

I explained to the company in Dochy's own words the reason he wouldn't be joining us in drink and watched the faces as the implications dawned of Dochy's previously closely guarded secret.

Other people have angina, but not the late, lamented, lovely Dochy.

John Fraser, former Scottish Farmer photographer

Many people think journalists write the headlines. This is not the case as the headline writing is left to the sub or page editor. This can lead to all sorts of misunderstandings. Thus an article on the importance of Basic Slag as a fertiliser was headed "Slag makes a comeback." The general public was surprised to see such a subject appearing on the farming pages.

Anon

An MSP attends a primary school visit to a farm at the end of which one boy appears to be missing. So the farmer checks out the steading and finds the boy up to his armpits in the midden, modelling something with his hands.

"Whit are ye daein' son?" asks the farmer. "Makin' a model o' a fairmer" comes the reply.

"An whit's that ye're usin' son?" inquires the farmer.

"Ah'm usin' s**te!!" says that boy abruptly.

The farmer is appalled at the boy's cheek and hurries off to find the teacher who, when told of the incident says, "Och, that'll be young Willie. He's aye up to mischief. Just leave it to me."

He heads off to the midden where he finds Willie still up to his armpits. "Hello Willie," says the teacher, "What're ye daein' son?"

Makin a model o' a teacher," comes the instant response.

"An what's that ye're usin Willie?" asks the teacher.

"Ah'm usin' s**te!" retorts Willie.

At this, the teacher is taken aback and tells Willie that he's in big trouble, because an important politician is also on the school farm visit.

On being told the circumstances, the MSP says, "Well, I'm used to dealing with tricky situations, and I think I can cope with young Willie. Leave it to me." And he also heads off to the midden in which Willie is still immersed.

When he gets there, he just stands and watches Willie for a while, as if assessing what the boy is up to, while Willie carries on modelling without a care in the world. Eventually the MSP speaks, "Ah Willie, I think I know what you're up to. You're making a model of a politician aren't you?" he asks in a rather self-satisfied manner.

"Ah'm bluidy sure ah'm no," comes the immediate reply. "Ah hivnae got hauf enough s**te fer that."

Alex Fergusson, MSP

FIVE

The farmer's wife brought a very limp duck into a veterinary surgeon. As she laid her pet on the table, the vet pulled out his stethoscope and listened to the bird's chest. After a moment or two, the vet shook his head and sadly said, "I'm sorry, your duck, Cuddles, has passed away."

The distressed woman wailed, "Are you sure?"

"Yes, I am sure. Your duck is dead," replied the vet.

"How can you be so sure?" she protested. "I mean you haven't done any testing on him or anything. He might just be in a coma or something. "

The vet rolled his eyes, turned around and left the room. He returned a few minutes later with a black Labrador Retriever. As the duck's owner looked on in amazement, the dog stood on his hind legs, put his front paws on the examination table and sniffed the duck from top to bottom. The dog then looked up at the vet with sad eyes and shook his head. The vet patted the dog on the head and took it out of the room.

A few minutes later he returned with a cat. The cat jumped on the table and also delicately sniffed the bird from head to foot. The cat sat back on its haunches, shook its head, meowed softly and strolled out of the room.

The vet looked at the woman and said, "I'm sorry, but as I said, this is most definitely, 100% certifiably, a dead duck."

The vet turned to his computer terminal, hit a few keys and produced a bill, which he handed to the woman.

The duck's owner, still in shock, took the bill. "£150!" she cried, "£150 just to tell me my duck is dead."

The vet shrugged, "I'm sorry. If you had just taken my word for it, the bill would have been £20, but with the Lab report and the Cat scan, it's now £150."

Anon

The tractor salesman was going his rounds when he saw a sight he had never seen before on his patch. There was a bull pulling a plough. He quickly saw an opportunity for a tractor sale and drove up the farm road.

Seeing the farmer, he pitched in with, "I reckon you could do with a tractor."

The old farmer just looked at him and then took the salesman round to a big shed and opened the doors. There was a tractor in pristine condition sitting there.

"But why have you got your bull pulling the plough?" the salesman asked.

"It is just to remind him that his life is not all pleasure," came the reply.

Michael Steel, St Andrews

The farmer's daughter had invited her new boyfriend to tea for the first time. Worried about the way her father spoke she asked her mother to be sure that he said 'fertiliser' rather than 'manure'. "I will try my best," said her mother, "But it has taken me twenty years to get him to say 'manure'."

George Burgher, formerly Orkney & Shetland NFUS secretary

Geordie was a lorry driver who spent his spare time working on farms. He had a passion for football and went on the famous Wembley trip in 1977; the one where the Scots broke the goalposts and brought the pitch home.

Along with his pals, they hired a minibus that was only doing about 10 miles to the bottle and which was driven by an agricultural worker from Cairngaan Farm, Drummore.

In the euphoric, alcoholic haze that was the post-match party in Trafalgar Square, the driver, worryingly, was nowhere to be seen. After a short discussion with the boys, Geordie was detailed to ask a policeman.

And so it was that Geordie approached one of the Met's finest with the immortal words: "Hae ye seen the dairyman fae Cairngaan?"

Alec Ross, Stranraer

Blood testing cattle was the bread and butter of farm vet practice over the summer months filling time after more pressured days of calving and lambing. It perhaps was a less welcome chore for farmers and crofters who had to bring cows back in to satisfy a relentless testing regime.

The routine work was not only an excuse to drive across wonderful landscapes; a window into numerous cattle herds and systems but also a chance to catch up with clients and friends. Crofters' cows still were often tied in byres, some of modern construction but many traditional cobbled, dim light and warm soft atmosphere heavy with the aroma of cows. Alison's byre was spotless and the cows stood content and still as she whispered to them. As the tail was lifted and the blood welled up in the vacutainer the animals hardly moved. The needle slipped out and the skin rubbed close before a needle change and a move down the line. Testing well behaved cows in a byre is a strangely relaxing and comfortable experience compared to the rush through crushes in bigger herds. Reading numbers on worn metal tags in the half light as cows shake their heads on their chains is a less rewarding part of the process! Alison's records however came to the rescue and we left the cows at peace to fill in the identification detail in the house over a cup of tea. That perhaps was not too unusual, and indeed testing 5 or 6 herds a day might mean 5 or 6 six teas and perhaps 2 or three whiskies before heading home late! The tea and scones were the real priority but at last we got on to filling in Rosie's details; unlike other cattle records hers consisted of matchboxes with each cows name on. Inside Rosie's box was a new shining never been used tag -SU BS 1163. Joyce also had a tag neatly boxed and labelled and so on. I filled in the testing sheets; the system had much to recommend it but I suspect would have not been to the liking of the men from the Ministry; I think Alison felt my unease at this form of identification so she explained that her system avoided the discomfort of puncturing the cows' ears and avoided tags getting lost. I signed the testing sheet and had to agree it was a fine system.

Nigel Miller, Stow, past president NFUS

A few years ago, a Perthshire farmer was asked to judge a Young Farmers speechmaking competition at the Eden Park Hotel, Cupar. He had had a busy day and had left home without having his tea. Getting to Cupar, he realised he was ahead of schedule and also that he was very hungry. Time for some tea, he thought, as he saw the Eden Park sign and dashed through the doors and along a corridor to where he heard voices. It was a dining room with tables all laid out. A couple of elderly ladies still having tea at one of them.

A young girl in uniform came up to him as he seated himself at an empty table and asked if she could help. "Can I have something to eat before the meeting starts?" he asked, adding he would be happy with a fish supper.

"Just a minute," she replied and disappeared into the kitchen, returning with an older uniformed lady.

"Can we help?" came the question and the farmer repeated he was just looking for something to eat before the meeting started.

"We have no meeting here. This is the Eden Park Old Folks home. You may be looking for the hotel further up the road."

Exit John McLaren, the embarrassed farmer.

John McLaren, Methven

Back in 1970, the NFU presidents for England, Northern Ireland and Scotland were out for lunch together when an annoying bluebottle flew in. Henry Plumb held up his knife and cut the fly in half. A housefly flew in and the Irish President cut it into quarters with his knife. When a midge flew in Andrew Arbuckle swiped it, but it flew on. When he was told that he could have done better Andrew stated, "That midge won't breed again and he will tell all midges not to meddle with the Scots in future."

George Burgher, formerly Orkney & Shetland NFUS secretary

Citizen's Band radio could be addictive. One tractor driver, Sandy used to spend his whole morning chattering away to others on all the activities in the neighbourhood. Come lunchtime, he would dash back to his house where he had a home set on which the local gossip continued to be exchanged.

One day, he had new callers at lunch time. They claimed they were nurses at a local hospital. Soon they were asking him about his job and then about his boss. Sandy told them all about his ploughing and then described working for his boss John. All was good until they asked him about the other workers on the farm. Soon, the so called nurses heard themselves being described in less than glowing terms. They called off and left a note for Sandy on his tractor seat. "Love from the nurses." He never used the CB radio again.

John Arbuckle

A farmer meets his friend in the street with a beautiful young lady hanging on to his arm and he introduces her as his new wife. He said she is wonderful, keeps the house spotless and always has his meals on the table on time and is fantastic in bed.

The man took his friend aside and asked, "How did you manage that?" and he replied, "I lied about my age. I said I was ninety five."

Jack Lawson, Cattle Improvement Service

After attending a meeting in the North of Scotland, Maitland Mackie was on the road home when he fancied a white pudding supper. He marched into the shop before realising he had no money to pay for his supper. He dashed out to his car to see if there was any cash in the pockets or the ash trays. He found not a penny but, nothing daunted, he marched back into the shop with a packet of new golf balls and traded them for his supper.

Gavin Dick, AHDB and formerly manager at Mackies

I was 23 years old when I attended my first NFU meeting in Avoch. An old stager asked me, "So what are you going to do on the farm?"

I answered, "Grow potatoes."

He replied, "Great crop potatoes, you've always got something to worry about."

Jamie Grant, Roskill

The now defunct Jarman's Hotel was directly opposite the cattle market in Forfar, making its location ideal for NFU meetings. It was a strictly commercial establishment however and specialised in hearty but heavily fried food. No one knew what colour the original décor had been but by the era when the meetings were held, it was nicotine brown.

This writer kept an old sports jacket exclusively for Jarman's meetings. Years later when it came to be thrown out, it still retained that pervasive aroma of overheated cooking fat and stale cigarette smoke.

Ewan Pate Courier

A shepherd was tending his sheep when a young man in BMW drove up the track. "If I can tell the exact number of sheep in your flock can I have one?" he asked. The shepherd agreed. Having consulted his laptop, scanned the area and used his GPS the young man said, "You have exactly 1,875 sheep."

As the number was correct the young man selected one of the sheep and took it into his car.

"Now," said the shepherd, "If I can guess what your job is can I have my animal back?" The young man agreed and the shepherd said, "You are a management consultant."

"How did you guess that correctly?"

"That was very easy. You come here uninvited, want to be paid for information that I already know, to a question that I never asked, and you know nothing about my business. Now give me my dog back."

George Burgher, formerly Orkney & Shetland NFUS secretary

The farmer was fast asleep at three o' clock in the morning when the doorbell went. He looked out of the window and there was a man who obviously had had a drink or two. "Can you give me a push?" the visitor asked. "No go away," replied the farmer shutting the window.

Returning to bed, his wife chastised him for not helping the stranger. "Do you not remember when we were stuck in that gateway and we had to get help?"

The farmer put his clothes on and went out the door shouting "Where are you? I have come to give you a push."

The stranger's voice came back. "I am round in the garden sitting on the children's swing."

Jim Webster, Dunkeld

Aberdeenshire farmers recall 1988 with horror as the weather during the summer and autumn was atrocious. There was clearly a need for the NFUS president, Ian Grant, to hear at first-hand how bad the job was. The meeting place was in a hotel at Auchnagatt where the crowd was such that an excited member of the press phoned his office for a photographer as the "fairmers were hingin on the rafters." There were only two seats left in the hall by the time the president and his chief executive, Scott Johnston arrived and these were beside a small window. As any good lieutenant would, Johnston looked out the window and assured his president that if all went badly, there was an escape route.

However, before the meeting started, the hotel manageress made an announcement. "Would the owner of car registration number xxxx please remove it as it is blocking an entrance."

Recognising the number as a new one, Grant stood up and said that it could not be as bad as it was made out as at least one member had a new car. This off the cuff remark broke the ice, even if it did not solve the problem.

Sir Ian Grant, former NFUS president

The dreaded wages inspector had called to check that everyone on the farm was being paid at or above the minimum wage rate.

"'I need a list of your employees and how much you pay them," he demanded of the farmer.

"Well, there's my tractorman who's been with me for 3 years. I pay him £400 a week plus he gets his house. Then there is the shepherd. He has done two lambings for me now and he gets £350 per week as well as his house and an allowance for his dogs," replied the farmer.

"Is that all the people on the farm?" asked the inspector.

"There's the half-wit who works about 18 hours every day and does 90% of all the work. In good times, he makes about £100 per week but pays for his own accommodation."

"That's the guy I want to talk to," says the agent.

"That would be me," replied the farmer.

Anon

A new orraman had been fee'd and it so happened the farmer was going to the mart the day the new employee started work.

At yolking time the farmer showed the orraman a newly harrowed field and said he wanted the stones lifted off before seeding.

The farmer emphasised that "a job well planned is a job half done." In this case that meant the stones should be gathered into heaps before taking the tractor into the field. He then rushed off to the mart for a busy day.

Getting home from the mart just before lousing time, the farmer asked his new orraman how he had got on with the stone gathering.

"Weel I'm half done."

"Oh that's great, 'cause it's a big field," said the farmer

"Aye I'm half done. I've planned where I am going to put the heaps."

Colin Mitchell, St Andrews

On a crowded Aberdeen steam enthusiasts' express, a young farmer walked the entire length of the train looking for a seat before realizing that the only seat available was currently occupied by a well-dressed, middle-aged English woman's poodle.

The weary young farmer asked, "Excuse me, may I have this seat?"

The English woman just sniffed, and said to no one in particular, "You Scots are so rude. My little Fifi is using the seat."

The young farmer walked the entire length of the train again and discovered that the only seat available was in fact the one occupied by the poodle.

Trudging tiredly back, he arrived once more in front of the English woman and said, "Please, may I sit down? I'm very tired."

She snorted, "Not only are you Scots rude, you are also arrogant. Why should I care if you are tired?"

This time, the young farmer didn't say a word, but simply picked up the little dog and tossed it out of the window and then sat down.

The woman shrieked, "Someone, defend my honour! This young man needs to be put in his place!"

An older Scottish landed gentleman sitting nearby spoke up, "Sir, you youngsters seem to have a penchant for doing the wrong thing. You vote for the wrong party; you marry for love and now, laddie, you appear to have thrown the wrong bitch out of the window!"

Bruce Jobson, Morpeth

After 14 years working with cattle and sheep in Aberdeenshire, I was hanging up my stethoscope to head south to work as a veterinary advisor for a drug company. Sad to leave, I invited vets, farmers and staff to my leaving party in a hotel near Duthie Park. One of the vets made a speech, a vet nurse read out a poem she had written for me and one farmer cried out, 'Bit Kate, there's nae coos in Londin ye ken'

Kate Richards, London

The old crofter was leaning over the dry stane dyke surveying his little patch of ground when an American tourist drew up. He was looking for his ancestral home but the big mouthed Texan could not contain his self-importance. "Back home," he said, "I can set off in the morning and by night fall, I will not have managed to ride round my ranch."

The reaction to this piece of boasting was less than enthusiastic. "I used to have a horse like that as well," replied the crofter.

David Jack, Gateside'

Reporter interviewing a 100 year old crofter.

Reporter: "Can you give us some health tips for reaching the age of 100?" Crofter: "For better digestion I drink beer. In the case of appetite loss I drink white wine. For low blood pressure I drink red wine. In the case of high blood pressure I drink whisky and when I have a cold I drink brandy." Reporter: "When do you drink water?"

Crofter: "I've never been that sick."

Gilmour Lawrie, Queensland

As chairman of the Parent Council of the small rural school of Morebattle in the Scottish Borders along with one of the teachers, I run an "Equestrian Club" once a month where both children with ponies and those who are just interested can come along and learn about various subjects including grooming, tack, the Countryside Code and different equestrian disciplines.

At a recent Parents' meeting one of the new mummies in the school said that she was delighted when her six year old daughter came home with the news that she had joined a new club at school. The mummy in question was amazed that a small school like Morebattle was doing debating for 6 year olds. It turns out her daughter had told her that she'd joined a 'Questioning Club.'

Gillian R McFadyen, The Borders Training Group

A tough old sheep farmer from Scotland gave some good advice to his granddaughter. He told her that the secret to a long life was to sprinkle a pinch of gunpowder onto her porridge every morning.

The granddaughter followed this dictum religiously until her death at the venerable age of 103.

She left behind 14 children, 30 grandchildren, 45 great grandchildren, 25 great great grandchildren and a forty foot hole where the crematorium used to be.

Jim Walker, Argent Energy and former president NFUS

Two Orkney farmers were out sea fishing and one of them became so seasick that he not only lost his tea but also his lower set of false teeth. However, they were determined to carry on with the fishing. The other farmer thought he would play a trick and took out his lower set of false teeth before secretly tying them to his friend's fishing hook.

The first farmer was excited by his catch and took the false teeth off the hook. Then he put the set in his mouth before quickly taking them out and studying them carefully.

"That's certainly no my teeth," he said before throwing them into the sea.

George Burgher, formerly Orkney & Shetland NFUS secretary

During the 1970s, we employed fourteen and fifteen year old schoolboys to rogue our cereal crops for blackgrass, wild oats and other weeds. One summer, they arrived with forms supplied by the Education Authority. The forms had to be signed by their headmaster, their parents and by their employer.

This was done and, in due course, a form came back allowing the youngster to work. The form said "xx was authorised to work and his work would be "sowing wild oats."

John Stevenson, Luffness Mains, former chairman, RSABI

SIX

A farmer was going by sleeper train to the Smithfield show and he was in the upper bunk bed. At Newcastle a nice looking blonde came in and went into the lower bunk. After some time the girl complained that she was cold and asked if he could get her a blanket. There was no response and she asked again if he could get her a blanket. There was still no action and after some time she said, "Would you like to pretend that we're married?" "Certainly," said the farmer, "Away and get your own bloody blanket."

George Burgher, formerly Orkney & Shetland NFUS secretary

It has been claimed that at Lanark Mart during the Ram Sales the Blackface breeders spill more drink in the bar than is actually consumed by their equivalents at the Texel Sale.

Anon

An Irish farmer's son called Neil Dunn went to London but did not write to his parents. When a neighbour was going to London on holiday they asked him to see if he could find their son who was living in the WC1 area of London. When the neighbour flew into London Airport he noticed a door with WC1 on it. He tried the first door but it was locked. He knocked on the door and said, "Are you Neilly Dunn?" "Yes," was the reply, "but I don't have any paper."

"That's no excuse for not writing to your parents in Ireland."

George Burgher, formerly Orkney & Shetland NFUS secretary

The scene is the annual dinner of the Institute of Auctioneers and Appraisers. Much libation has been taken. The mood is good. The guest speaker, flanked at the top table by the chairman and the secretary, rises to address the audience. He speaks and speaks and speaks. The audience begins to grow impatient, enough is enough – auctioneers by profession want to get to the point quickly.

A disgruntled member of the audience picks up a half empty bottle of red wine and hurls it at the speaker, but hits the chairman squarely on the forehead. As he slumps beneath the table, he is heard to utter the memorable and heartfelt words, "Hit me again, I can still hear the blighter."

Bill Howatson, formerly Press & Journal

The auctioneer was on his annual round of canvassing for the store sales and after exchanging introductory civilities on one Aberdeenshire farm, he asked the farmer how his wife was.

"Oh she died last month," was the reply. The auctioneer expressed his sorrow and then moved on to getting the cattle.

A year later, he was back up the same farm road but had forgotten what he had been told. During the introductions, he asked the farmer how his wife was keeping.

"She died last year," came the rather dry reply. However, the two men went on to make a deal supplying cattle to the store sale.

Another twelve months passed but this time the farmer spied the auctioneer coming up the farm road. Before the visitor could say anything, the farmer blurted out, "And before you ask about the wife, she is still deid."

Willie Porter, West Scryne

The late Dave Lawson, potato merchant in Kirriemuir, was not a lover of committees. "They spend time taking minutes and waste hours."

Deryk Smith, Cupar

Maitland's father, Sir Maitland Mackie, used to tell this story against himself. When he finished university and came home to the farm, his job in the morning was to milk the cows and then join the rest of the men on the farm in whatever the task of the day was. On this occasion it was pooin' neeps (pulling turnips). Maitland joined the squad and for something to say, remarked "Aye, gie caul' on the fingers this mornin'." To which the grieve quickly responded: "Well, dinna haud on to them sae lang!"

Eddie Gillanders, Farm North East

In the days of Cupar market, one of the favourite meeting and eating places was the Royal Hotel. One day, the old farmer went in for his lunch and ordered boiled ham.

This duly appeared but the customer was not impressed. "Who cut the ham?" he asked the waiter. "I did," came the reply.

"Well you damn near missed it," said the unhappy diner.

Peter Small, Falfield

My dad was always keen to involve himself with the workings of the sheep flock despite many days away with the 'Council.' Gathering the ewes and lambs in July to shear the ewes was always a social highlight that involved an early start to get the ewes off the high hill before it got too hot. Having gathered the mob together, there was a break for a "midser" before driving them the long trail back to the farm. Usually the 'herds carried a 'piece' prepared the night before, but in this occasion my dad had hurriedly put together his own 'piece' as he had his breakfast just before he left the house. So it was that he got his bag, took out the roll and tried to break the shell off the recently boiled egg before surreptitiously placing it back in his bag.

His efforts had not gone un-noticed and a quiet comment from old Calum alerted all to the farmer's shortcomings. "Aye, aye. I'm saying, there's no' much nourishment in a cheena egg."

He was often reminded of the day he boiled the china egg for his picnic.

Ian Duncan Millar, Tirinie

We had a new bank manager who, although not from an agricultural background, was keen to meet the local farming community and get out to see life on the farms. My father invited him up at lambing time and so one night he arrived and I got him to pull out a few lambs – all successfully. The following day was his half-day and so he came back up, this time bringing his wife to prove that he had indeed acquired some new skills.

Our system is simple; ewes inside at night and outside through the day and, when walking round the lambing field, I was able to give a brief history of the individual ewes that had lambed and how they had performed in previous years. He stopped and looked round the field of several hundred Greyface ewes and said, "Now, how do you know all these sheep? They all look much the same to me."

I replied, "I don't, but I know the good ones and I know the bad ones. The ones in the middle I don't know at all."

"Ah" he exclaimed, "Same as in the bank!"

Robert Barr, Woodhouse

When I was a young loon at the Old Market in Perth at an October bull sales, a certain Charolais breeder approached me as I leaned against the bull pens. He was a man whom my father didn't particular like due to his miserableness! He said to me in a grunting manner, "Does yer bull kick?" I said "No, he's a quiet bull" so he moved forward and touched the bull on the tail head. Immediately the bull lashed out kicking the said gentleman in a rather delicate area. He shouted out at me in a strained way, "I thought your bull didn't kick?"

I said he doesn't. He's in the next pen.

Andrew Hornall, Falleninch

A tale from the early days of Artificial Insemination where the procedures were not fully understood. The AI man arrived at the small dairy and the recipient cow identified. The farmer's wife then helpfully pointed out, "There's a nail to hing yer breeks on."

Anon

Farmers understanding computers:

1. Log on: when you want to make the farmhouse warmer.
2. Lap top: where the cat sleeps.
3. Hard drive: manoeuvring through rocky outcrops when there is snow in the ground.
4. Windows: what to shut when it's cold outside.
5. Byte: what midgies do.
6. Modem: what they do to the hay fields.
7. Keyboard: where the keys hang.
8. Mouse: vermin that eat grain.

Anon

A feed rep visited a farm. The farmer said to him, 'Wait in the lounge I'll just wash my hands'. The rep rushed back shouting. There was a major problem. There was a bull in the lounge.

"Oh aye," said the farmer, "That's old Darkness. Since artificial insemination came in he's got nothing to do and he just wanders about. He often comes in to watch the tele. He likes watching the cricket best."

"Is he safe?" asked the rep.

"Oh aye," said the farmer. "The only time you've got to watch is when the tele goes off and the message appears. Normal service will be resumed as soon as possible."

Bob Noble, formerly Duns and Borders NFU

Many years ago, in the old stockmen's huts at the Highland Show a young Scottish farmer was in a clinch with a young lady stockswoman from Wales. In deep embrace she said, "I know what you want. You want my knickers round my ankles."

Although taken aback by the comment, the young man replied, "Correct."

She then said "Just a minute then till I get them out of my bag."

Anon

Aubin Roger of Rumgally Farm, Cupar delighted to retell an occasion at a War Executive committee meeting when his great uncle, Frank Roger, had raised the problem of serious rabbit damage to grain crops and the need for much more trapping assistance at his Peekie Farm, Boarhills.

The chairman enquired of Frank how many rabbits might be involved, to which he replied, "Dozens".

His brother Charles Roger from Rumgally corrected, "No there were hundreds last time I was along at Peekie."

Their old father had not heard the remarks and asked for them to be repeated after which he stated, "No, thousands."

Sandy Millar, consultant formerly SAI

When Major Ian Campbell was NFUS President he came to visit the Banff Area. We took him on a visit to Glenlivet. Included in the itinerary, in addition to farm visits, we visited a couple of well-known distilleries. The afternoon wore on and we had a bite to eat in Tomintoul when the President thought he should phone Michael Joughin of Moray Area to say he was behind schedule and would not be able to join him at Elgin for a meal before the meeting. An hour later he phoned to say he might be slightly late in getting to the meeting at which he was supposed to speak for half an hour on co-operation. Next day I learned that when he arrived at the meeting, he spoke for an hour and a half and never mentioned co-operation.

Alan Meldrum, formerly NFUS Banff

After a Westray funeral, two farmers were coming out of the kirkyard discussing their ages. The older one said, "A'm ninety five the morn."

Expressing surprise the younger man said, "It's hardly worth thee while gan home."

George Burgher, formerly Orkney & Shetland NFUS secretary

A North-east farmer and keep fit enthusiast - they are not mutually exclusive - checked into a Hyde Park hotel in London for the Royal Smithfield Show. He asked the receptionist if the hotel had a gym as he liked to get up early in the morning to do his exercises which, in order to derive the maximum benefit from them, he did in the nude. The receptionist informed him that the hotel had no gym but if he was out early in the morning, he should just go across to Hyde Park to do his exercises - there would be nobody about at that time of the morning.

So he's out early the next morning, completely starkers. A couple of rounds of jogging and finishing, as he always did, with 50 press ups. He's really struggling to make the 50 and pechin and panting - 46, 47... at which point a late night reveller appears on the scene on his way back from Stringfellows and still in his pin-striped suit and bowler hat. He looks at this apparition on the grass moving his body up and down painfully slowly. Poking him in the ribs with his brolly, he slurs: "Scuse me, my man. I think the lady's got fed up and gone home!"

Eddie Gillanders, Farm North East

My first introduction into pedigree stock was at Balmoral, Belfast where United Auctions conducted sales of pedigree pigs. The sale attracted its fair share of characters and it was a great learning ground for a young auctioneer.

A notable incident was around the sale of a boar owned by the colourful Robert Overend. He was a master salesman who always had a story. This particular boar had no tail. Robert went to great lengths to advise that the condition was not genetic and it was due to being cut off accidentally in the trailer door while loading the animal.

After the usual long selling process the boar was successfully sold for 800 guineas. Robert asked me to point out the bidder to whom he proceeded to present the decomposing tail.

David Leggat, United Auctions

Maitland Mackie had to attend a meeting in London. He took one of the Mackie company cars to Aberdeen airport and, as the meeting was to be short and as he was booked on a return flight later that day, he left it in the short stay car park. On the flight home, he met an old friend and they had a dram or two. The friend who was being collected at the airport offered to give Maitland a lift home and this was duly accepted.

Two months passed and the car was forgotten until the Mackie's book keeper was doing a stock take and found out there was a missing car.

Maitland said nothing but quietly went to the airport next day, paid the hundreds of pounds of short stay car parking charges and surreptitiously returned the vehicle

Gavin Dick, AHDB and formerly manager at Mackies

Three sheep farmers met up with three dairy farmers in a railway station. The dairy farmers all bought a ticket each for the journey but the sheep farmers only bought one for the three of them.

When the farmers got on the train the three sheep farmers all crushed into one of the toilets. When the ticket collector came along he knocked on the door of the toilet and asked for "tickets please". The door opened a little bit and a hand appeared with a ticket in it. The ticket collector punched a hole in the ticket and handed it back.

The next day the farmers met at the same place but this time the three dairy farmers only bought one ticket between the three of them. Surprisingly the sheep farmers didn't buy any tickets at all.

Once inside the train the three dairy farmers all piled into one of the toilets and waited for the ticket collector.

One of the sheep farmers went up to the door and knocked and asked for "tickets please".

Neale McQuistin, Airyolland

The young loon asks the farmer he's working for if he could borrow a lantern. The farmer asks him what he's needing it for. "Oh," says the young loon. "Am gaen coortin'." The farmer laughs: "Michty me, when I was coortin, I didnae need a lantern." "No," says the young loon. "An' look fit ee landed wi!"

Eddie Gillanders, Farm North East

Angus NFU Area always used to meet on a Monday afternoon. The timing was perfect, allowing time for members to trade stock at Scott and Graham's weekly sale. After a bite of lunch they could then settle down for an afternoon of agri-political debate and then head off for home in time to have a chat with the grieve as to how the day's work had progressed.

By the mid 1980s, there was a problem. There were no farm grieves and not even many men. The younger Area members no longer had time for a leisurely day in Forfar and moved that the meetings should be held in the evenings. The debate was intense. George Galloway, East Balmirmer was strongly against the change, arguing that a professional association should conduct its business in working hours.

Jim Steel from Craignathro, just outside Forfar, was as loyal an NFUS member as could be found anywhere but he was also a great wag. "Evening meetings will do fine as long as I can watch Emmerdale before I leave home!" he said.

Soap opera or not, eventually the matter came to a vote and lo and behold, the ballot was exactly evenly split. The chairman was bracing himself for the casting vote when someone noticed that James Black, Backboath had fallen asleep. He was given a rude awakening, had the position explained to him and with commendable alacrity voted for the evening meetings.

Ewan Pate, Courier

Friends of a candidate for the NFU presidency were canvassing feverishly on pre-election night. At midnight they gathered in his hotel room and assured him, "You've got the support of all thinking farmers."

"No good," he groaned, holding his head in his hands. "I need a majority."

Fordyce Maxwell

SEVEN

A crofter in Orkney is sitting on a dyke on a richt fine day. For no real reason he has a few dry rabbits turdies which he is playing with when a big loud Texan, complete with a stetson hat came along. With uncommon politesse the tourist said, "Good day to you sir. My Gaad, you've got a beautiful country. Excuse me for asking but what's that you've got there?" "Och it's just some intelligence pills."

"Wow. That's something. Can I buy some?"

"Och aye. You can have three for a fiver. We like our pills to go where they are most needed."

So the deal was done. The tourist wasted no time and popped two of the pills into his mouth. Almost at once the American's look of savour turned to alarm.

"Jeese man! These pills are sh*t."

"Aye, there you go," said the man of Orkney. "They're workin' already."

Charlie Allan, author and raconteur

An Orkney farmer's son was sent out by his mother to fetch a bucket of water from the well. En route to the well he met a friend going to Kirkwall and he decided to go there too. In Kirkwall he went to the harbour where he was offered a job on a boat going to Leith. In Leith he decided to join a boat going to Australia. After about a year he became homesick and decided to return to Orkney. When he came through the door his mother was sitting on a stool in front of the fire knitting a pair of socks. After he announced his presence, she stood up, turned round and said, "Where's the pail o' water?"

George Burgher, formerly Orkney & Shetland NFUS secretary

At a Forth Valley NFU area meeting, Gavin Millar, Plean, was giving a fulsome report as the representative on the Union's Potato committee. This was too much for dairy farmer, John Paterson, Woodend, Balfron who interrupted, "Just tell us how much we will have to pay for brock* this year."

*Brock are the potatoes not fit for human consumption but valued as stock feed.

Andrew Arbuckle

Ernie was a sheltered young man who worked on a farm near Cupar in the 1950s. He had never ventured far from Cupar so one day his boss said, "Ernie, why don't you take a day off and visit Edinburgh". So Ernie duly took the train through to the big city. The day after, his boss asked him, "So how did it go Ernie?"

I got on fine boss, it was braw, but I didnae ken it was covered in gless."

It turns out, he hadn't managed to get out of Waverly station.

Andrew Duncan, Buckler

Speaking at the Aberfeldy Branch AGM, as I was introduced to the chairman, Sandy Thomson, I burst out laughing which is not the best way to garner votes. I promised to explain in my speech. I told the members that I was often introduced to chairmen and sometimes struggled to remember their names later in the night. There was no chance of this happening on this occasion.

On a study tour of farms in France, the farmers sat down to a meal with their French hosts. One Aberdonian sat opposite a French farmer who wished him "Bon appétit." The Aberdonian replied, "Sandy Thomson". The evening meal went the same way, with the Frenchman again saying "Bon appétit". The Scotsman replied "Sandy Thomson". He began to suspect something was not quite right, and made a few enquiries.

The next day, he made sure he was seated opposite the same Frenchman, and got in first with a hearty "Bon appétit". The Frenchman replied "Sandy Thomson!"

Peter Stewart, Urquhart

The old farmer gave his workers half an egg for breakfast every morning. Tired of this parsimony, one employee left the table and went outside. The old farmer went out to look for him and found him standing among the hens. The farmer asked him what he was doing.

He replied, "I am looking for the hen that's laying that half egg."

Martha and Ramsay Sykes, Coylton

David Wilson, Balmullo, who won the world horse shoe championship in 1985 tells of when he needed a new apprentice. The youth arrived escorted by both parents. During the interview, his mother stated he had never done any hard work in his life so he would be "just full of it." The boy got the job and proved to be a good blacksmith.

David Wilson, Balmullo

Dan was a single farmer's son living at home with his father and working in the family business. He found out he was going to inherit the farm when his sickly father died, so he decided he needed to find a wife with whom to share his fortune.

One evening, in a pub in Edinburgh, he spotted the most beautiful woman he had ever seen. Her natural beauty took his breath away.

"I may look like just an ordinary guy," he said to her, "but in just a few years, my father will die and I will inherit farms worth £20 million."

Impressed, the woman asked for his business card and three days later, she became his stepmother.

Women are so much better at financial planning than men.

Jim Walker, Argent Energy and former president NFUS

Various livestock auction companies hold sales of horses and ponies. Often because these sales involve selling a well loved family pet, there can be more emotion than is normal at a sheep or cattle sale. At one pony sale as the pony trotted around the ring, the mother of the family selling it urged the auctioneer to ensure it went to a good home. Bids were difficult to come by as the pony was not in the first flush of youth. However, the auctioneer did get a bidder.

"Is it going to a good home?" the mother asked.

"It is going to about 400 good homes…. in tins of dog food," the auctioneer replied under his breath.

Brian Henderson, Scotsman

A young Orkney farmer left home to go to Australia without telling anyone what he was going to do and he did not contact his parents while he was away. Years later, when he returned late one night his father asked him where he had been, to which he replied, "Oot."

George Burgher, formerly NFUS Orkney & Shetland

A Glasgow lawyer went duck hunting in rural Aberdeenshire.

He shot and dropped a bird, but it fell into a farmer's field on the other side of a fence. As the lawyer climbed over the fence, an elderly farmer drove up on his tractor and asked him what he was doing.

The litigator responded, "I shot a duck and it fell in this field, and now I'm going to retrieve it."

The old farmer Peter replied, "This is my property, and you are not coming over here."

The indignant lawyer said, "I am one of the best trial lawyers in Scotland and, if you don't let me get that duck, I'll sue you and take everything you own."

The old farmer smiled and said, "Apparently, you don't know how we settle disputes in Mintlaw. We settle small disagreements like this with the 'Three Kick Rule.'"

The lawyer asked, "What is the 'Three Kick Rule'?"

The Farmer replied, "Well, because the dispute occurs on my land, I get to go first. I kick you three times and then you kick me three times and so on back and forth until someone gives up."

The lawyer quickly thought about the proposed contest and decided that he could easily take the old codger. He agreed to abide by the local custom.

The old farmer slowly climbed down from the tractor and walked up to the lawyer.

His first kick planted the toe of his heavy steel-toed work boot into the lawyer's groin and dropped him to his knees.

His second kick to the midriff sent the lawyer's last meal gushing from his mouth.

The lawyer was on all fours when the farmer's third kick to his rear end, sent him face-first into a fresh cow pie.

Summoning every bit of his will and remaining strength the lawyer very slowly managed to get to his feet.

Wiping his face with the arm of his jacket, he said, "Okay, you old fart. Now it's my turn."

The old farmer smiled and said, "Nah, loon, I give up. Keep the duck."

Dave Balfour, Auchtermuchty

Dod was very proud of his farming and as he had a number of fields adjoining the A68, their appearance was very important. Imagine his consternation when he found a field full of drilling errors or it may have been weeds. What did the wily Dod do? He stuck four canes in the field and erected a sign near the road with the important message 'College Trials'.

David Cranstoun, retired SAC advisor

An old farmer overheard two guys in their mid-thirties while sitting at a bar.

One of the guys said to his mate, "Man you look tired."

His buddy said, "Dave, I'm exhausted. My girlfriend and I have sex all the time. I just don't know what to do."

The farmer offered the wisdom of years and said, "Marry her. That'll put a stop to that stuff!"

Dave Balfour, Auchtermuchty

This farmer from near New Luce was always in a hurry. His long suffering wife always complained. Many times with some justification, it must be said, that they never did anything together any more. So one Friday when he was selling cattle in Ayr, he took Jeanie with him. The idea was she could have had a day's shopping while he sold his cattle.

About teatime, a fellow farmer met him back in Stranraer.

"How was trade the day?"

"Aye, no' bad".

"That's good. How's Jeanie?"

There's a look of horror on the man's face.

"Damn it to hell!" he exclaims. "I HAE LEFT HER IN AYR!"

Alec Ross, Stranraer

The 2015 Royal Highland show proved to be one of the busiest ever – and the organisers revealed that virtually all of the show's 15,000 car-park spaces had been filled on the busiest day…

One of those was filled by an old farmer from Perthshire who, to save red faces, we shall call Wullie.

Now, sadly, Wullie's old Land Rover had broken down the day before the show and he had thought that he would miss out on his one day a year away from the farm. However, his son, who worked in the nearby town, kindly lent him his car for the day - allowing Wullie to make his annual pilgrimage to Ingliston.

He thoroughly enjoyed the show, meeting a lot of the friends he hadn't seen since the previous year, and extracting as many cups of tea from machinery salesman as the wafer-slim promise of "maybe managing some business" over the next 12 months could elicit.

However, despite having had a thoroughly good day - as those poor souls who manned the car park at the showground soon found out - come "head for home" time, Wullie had a problem.

He couldn't remember where he'd parked the car. In fact, as he'd got a bit lost on the way into the showground, he couldn't even remember which car park it was in.

And so a major search was launched to find Wullie's vehicle.

Now Wullie could remember that the car was a "sort of silver" colour and that it was a hatchback.

It might have been a Vauxhall Astra, equally it might have been a Ford Focus – or it might even have been "one of those Japanese jobs".

The parking attendants realised this wasn't going to be an easy job - and the only other thing Wullie could remember was the fact that it had a wee scratch on the driver's door, a "6" somewhere in the registration number and pair of wellies sitting in the boot.

The hunt was on - but even by the time that the car-park had thinned out to the straggle of late-night revellers, the ever-helpful attendants were still struggling to track down Wullie's transport.

Eventually, after hours of searching, the head attendant who was feeling sorry for this old farmer caught up with Wullie to explain the situation:

"We've really been struggling – and I'm afraid the only car left that fits your description has a rack of bright orange canoes tied to the roof," related the attendant.

"Oh, aye," said Wullie, "That's the one!"

Brian Henderson, Scotsman

When I was assessing on Uist, I had to visit a crofter who had some sheep and a fank* on a wee island about one hundred yards off shore when the tide was in, as it was on my visit.

He said he would row me across in his wee boat. After looking at the sheep and the fank on the island we went to his house to complete the paperwork. This was duly completed and as I was bidding my farewell he said, "It will be £1.50 for the ferry."

Johnny Morison, QMS Assessor

In a court in the North West of Scotland, the lawyer was cross examining the old farmer who claimed he had suffered injuries after his pony and trap had been in an accident.

"At the scene of the accident, McTavish did you not tell the Northern Constabulary officer that you had never felt better in your life?"

"That is correct, sir."

The lawyer then asked, "How is it that you are now claiming you were seriously injured when my client's car hit your cart?"

McTavish replied, "When the policeman arrived, he went over to my horse which had a broken leg, and shot him. Then he went over to Ben, my dog who was badly hurt, and shot him.

"So when he asked me how I felt, I just thought, under the circumstances, I would say I've never felt better in my life."

Anon

I never realised how addictive smoking could be until one day the old cattler on the farm was emptying the calf pens. This was warm work and he had hung his jacket on a hook as he wheeled the barrow onto the midden. Suddenly a gust of wind took the jacket off the peg and it landed in the pool of slurry at the foot of the midden. The old boy went to retrieve the now sodden jacket.

I said "You are not going to wear that are you?"

"No," he replied, "but my Woodbine* are in the pocket and I need a smoke."

*a particularly pungent brand of cigarettes

Andrew Arbuckle

After forty nine years of marriage with Betty, Bob Mitchell, Drumdreel, Strathmiglo, recalled their first meeting. "It was at a Young Farmers Dance in Stirling. She was sitting in a group of girls and I knew one of them was a secretary and assumed the rest of them were as well. However, following them upstairs to the dance hall, I noticed Betty had welly marks on her legs and thought "That will do me."

For those who may miss the significance of the welly marked legs, it meant she was used to working and especially working in the milking parlour.

Anon

The Aberdeenshire farmer had never skied before but his pals had told him it was good fun. So he booked a holiday in the French Alps. He had no gear but soon saw a shop where it could be bought and, more importantly, it had a sign saying "English spoken here."

Soon he was kitted out with boots but when the skies were laid out in front of him, he was perplexed. "Noo fit fit fits fit ski?" he asked.

The shop assistant who thought he knew English was also left perplexed.

John Whitehead, Largo

The arrival of the mobile phone changed farming communications. Some had tried short wave radio but it was all a bit clunky and full of "Roger and out" and stuff.

One early convert to mobile phones was an East Neuk of Fife farmer. He was baling straw one day with his mobile tucked in behind the tractor seat. The field was bumpy and he realised his phone must have bounced out. There was no sign of it on the ground so he went back to the farmhouse and asked his wife to keep ringing the mobile. This explains why his neighbours could see him running from bale to bale listening intently for the ring tones to give away the secret of where the phone had ended up.

Anon

EIGHT

It's no big secret that the fair sex have been putting men off their sleep for generations. An Angus farmer was walking along the beach at St Cyrus thinking of an old girlfriend when there in the sand he spotted a rusty lamp. He picked it up and rubbed it and a genie popped out.

The genie said, "Bloody hell, you're the fourth one this week. You can only have one wish."

Said the chap, "An old girl-friend of mine whom I haven't seen for many, many years now lives in America. I'm afraid of flying and terrified of sailing. Can you build me a bridge across the Atlantic?"

"Don't be silly," said the genie. "Think of all the steel or concrete we'd need and the planning permission - but I will relent. You can have one more wish."

"Thanks," said the man. "I've been married and divorced four times. Can you grant me the power to understand a woman? Tell me what makes her happy, what makes her sad?"

Said the genie, "See that bridge. Would you like two lanes or four?"

Arthur Anderson, formerly BBC Landward producer

In the 1800s many Orcadian farmers' sons went to work for the Hudson's Bay Company so that they could return home with enough capital to start their own businesses. After he had been in Canada for over twelve months one of the workers heard that his wife had had a son. His friend asked him if he wasn't worried about this, to which he replied, "Oh that's nothing. There's four years between my brother and me."

George Burgher, formerly Orkney & Shetland NFUS secretary

In the autumn of 1940 from time to time German bombers came up the Fife coast in an attempt to bomb the Forth Bridge. They had to be quick because there was a squadron of spitfires at RAF Turnhouse who were always keen to do battle with them.

One beautiful autumn afternoon we were lifting potatoes at Balbuthie ably assisted by a crowd of hard working women tattie pickers – mostly from Methil.

A raid on the Forth Bridge by some German bombers caused the usual retaliation by the Turnhouse Spitfires. In the ensuing dog fight a German bomber was shot down and the pilot bailed out of his stricken aircraft and parachuted gently down to land in the middle of the Methil women busy picking tatties.

The Methil women lost no time or opportunity of letting the German pilot know exactly what they thought of him. Five or six of them pinned him to the ground whilst the others kicked and stabbed him with a fork.

Grandfather, who was visiting the field at the time, and the grieve had to rush over and rescue the poor airman who was hurting badly from the 'Methil treatment'. The pilot was eventually tied up with 'sparty' rope and the police were summoned, but from time to time one of the tattie women would run over and give him another jab with the fork.

Eventually the police arrived, much to the relief of the poor pilot who was now bleeding profusely and his final question to my grandfather and grieve before he was led out of the field – delivered in broken English – was, "are all Scottish women like that?!"

John Cameron, Balbuthie

Two hens were watching a cock eyed cockerel at the other end of their pen. One said to the other, "We had better separate now or he will probably miss us both."

Sandy Scott, Dolphinston

An American in a large flashy American car stopped by the side of a Highland road to ask a farmer the way. The farmer pointed at the car and asked, "What's that?"

"That's my au-to-mob-ile," the American replied in a long Texan drawl. He then looked at the farmer's ancient implement hitched to the tractor. "What's that?"

"It ought-to-mow-hay" was the reply.

David Cranstoun, retired SAC advisor

While the farmer surveyed what was left after the fire in his barn, his wife rang the insurance company and asked them to send a cheque for £20,000, the sum that the barn was insured for. The claims official explained that they would not get the money, but that they would pay for replacing the barn. "In that case," said the wife, "cancel the policy I have on my husband."

George Burgher, formerly Orkney & Shetland NFUS secretary

An old farmer wins £5 million on the lottery and, when asked what he was going to do with the money, replies "I'll farm until I've spent it all".

Ian Williams, Campbell Dallas, Perth

A prominent North-east farmer and businessman, who was a noted womaniser, had a horse running at York and invited all his pals down to see the race. The horse won and he took all his pals for a sumptuous meal afterwards, along with the trainer who was a rather supercilious Englishman. As he leaned back in his chair with brandy glass in one hand and cigar in the other, the trainer said to the horse owner: "Well, James, once you get a bit of success in life, there are three things you need - a horse, a dog and a mistress. At which point one of James' pals shouted up the table: "Aye, Jimmy, a doot we'll hae to get ye a dog!"

Eddie Gillanders, Farm North East

Union vice president, Peter Stewart was speaking at a regional meeting when the chairman announced that the Union was going online with its own web-site. The chairman then offered the following view. "Your dear leader will be pictured and bear in mind, should you be tempted to put your foot through the screen, it is only your own equipment you are damaging."

Peter Stewart, Urquhart

A Borders farmer had two of the best tickets for the Rugby World Cup final. As he sat down, another man came along and asked if anyone was sitting next to him.

"No, the seat is empty."

"That is incredible. Who in their right mind would have a seat like this for the World Cup, one of the biggest sporting events of the year and not use it?"

The farmer then admitted the seat belonged to him. "My wife was supposed to come with me but she passed away. This will be the first Cup Final she will have missed since we were married."

"Oh I am sorry to hear that. That is terrible. I suppose you could not get anyone else, a friend, a relative or even a neighbour to take up the seat?"

The farmer shook his head. "No, they are all at her funeral."

Jim Walker, Argent Energy and former president NFUS

The late Dan Buglass used to tell this story about the jiggery pokery of stock judging although the originator of the tale might have been Ben Coutts. A poultry judge had chosen his winner as coming from Cage 21. When it was pointed out there was no bird in Cage 21, the judge was unabashed. "There soon will be," he responded.

Anon

The old shepherd found himself sitting at dinner next to very pretty lady wearing a lovely white dress. He managed fine with the soup and meat courses but when it came to the sweet course he was a bit baffled because it was cherries and custard.

"What would he do with the cherry stones?" he wondered. He decided to store them in the side of his mouth till he couldn't hold any more. Then he spat them into his plate causing the red cherry juice to splatter all over the lady's pretty white dress.

Though annoyed, the lady was very tactful and enquired if cherry stains came out?

"Och aye," said the shepherd, "I've swallowed hundreds o' them and they aye come oot."

Sandy Scott, Dolphinston

An elderly farmer had a large pond in his orchard. One evening, he decided to go down to the pond and he grabbed a twenty litre bucket to bring back some fruit. As he neared the pond, he heard voices shouting and laughing with glee. As he came closer, he saw it was a bunch of young women skinny dipping in his pool. He made the women aware of his presence and they all went to the deep end of the pool. One shouted at him, "We are not coming out until you leave."

The old man frowned and said, "I didn't come down here to watch you ladies swim naked or to make you get out of the pond naked. Holding up the bucket, he added, "I just came down here to feed the crocodile."

Jim Webster, Dunkeld

An NFU President was ill and the local Secretary went to visit him to inform him that the Branch Committee had passed a resolution wishing him a speedy recovery by a majority of 13 to 12.

George Burgher, formerly Orkney & Shetland NFUS secretary

The old farmer had died and his two sons were sitting in the solicitor's office waiting room readying themselves for the reading of their father's will.

The two started arguing over which of them was the favourite son. It was an argument that had been part of their life for years.

They were then invited into the office where, after a few preliminaries, the solicitor came to the important item; which one who would inherit the farm.

The solicitor took a deep breath and addressed the elder brother, "The farm is yours."

The older one turned to his brother and complained. "I told you that you were the favourite."

Anon

There was the farmer who, because of his "horses are thin, his corn is cheap an' his harness fairly dune" attitude was unloved by his workers.

However he was wealthy and fervently wished for real status. After twice standing for election to the County Council and failing, he sufficiently ingratiated himself locally and was invited to become a Justice of the Peace.

His reaction to this was predictable. He strutted about like a popinjay.

The morning after his installation, he appeared very early while the men were still getting ready for the day's work. Dressed immaculately with blue serge suit, highly polished brown boots and wearing his bowler hat he walked up and down the line of the stables and cart shed.

Not having been greeted, he looked around him and in a loud voice he declared, "I don't suppose any of you lads will have seen a JP before." "Nah," came a voice from down the line, "but I've seen a craw sh*ting."

Louis Flood, photographer, Perth

The press conference was well underway at this big hotel at Erskine. The late Dan Buglass lit up his pipe to help his concentration (smoking in public places was allowed in those days). Suddenly the fire alarm went off and we all scarpered out to join the several hundred other guests and residents on the lawn in front of the hotel. After half an hour, when the firemen had checked the premises, everybody was allowed back in.

"What was the problem?" we wondered.

"Somebody smoking in the conference room" we were told. Dan's pipe was still belching black reek, so to save another fire alarm, he was persuaded to douse the flames.

Andrew Arbuckle

On one of his grass seed selling trips to Northumberland, Johnny Watson felt unwell and went off to bed early; a most unusual occurrence for this noted bon viveur.

The next day, still feeling less than his normal perky self, he headed home where he was quizzed on whether he had been taking his normal medicine.

"Of course," he replied and produced a small medicine bottle from his pocket. He looked at the label, only to find out that in his haste to depart earlier in the week, he had mistakenly picked up pills belonging to the family dog.

He admitted to being dog tired but not to feeling inclined to chase sheep.

Johnny Watson, Watson Seeds

Two farmers had not met since they were together at school. After fifty years they met on the older one's farm and were discussing insurance cover. The farm was covered for fire, burglary, and earthquake. The visiting farmer said that he could understand the fire and burglary cover,

"But how on earth do you start an earthquake?"

George Burgher, formerly Orkney & Shetland NFUS secretary

A tale from the 1970's involving a student gaining work experience at everyone else's expense. Back then we were in a pea harvesting co-op with the men from all the member's farms manning the viners and the pea cutters. It was skilled work but we always had a student whose job was to run errands, help with breakdowns and so on. On this particular day I asked the student who was with us that year to take a tractor back to the field we had just left, to fetch the diesel bowser.

It was only about six miles away and we expected him back within the hour but three hours later, as the viners were running short of fuel, we realised the lad had not returned. Shortly, he did appear at the bottom of the field but he seemed to be having great difficulty steering the yoke, an MF 188, if I remember correctly, through the gate. Eventually he gave up and came stomping up the field to the waiting group. He was clearly in a dreadful temper. "Who is supposed to look after that tractor?" he stormed. "It is a bloody disgrace . The steering hardly works, it has taken me two hours to get back and I had to take eight cuts to get round the roundabout in Arbroath. There was queue a mile long behind me!"

The man whose tractor it was on a day- to- day to day basis stepped forward and calmly said; "Did you happen to put your foot on a little pedal at the side, by any chance?"

"I might have done," admitted the rapidly deflating youth. "Why would that make any difference?"

He had of course driven six miles with the differential lock on. Fortunately the tractor survived the experience none the worse apart from some rather badly scuffed tyres.

Ewan Pate, Courier

A farmer had a bull that a problem 'jumping' cows so the vet prescribed a course of tablets. A week or two later the farmer phoned the vet to say they seemed to be working but asked for another batch. The vet asked if he could remember the name of the tablets, to which the reply was, "I hae nae idea but they tasted like peppermint."

Alistair Donaldson, formerly Meat and Livestock Commission

Three farmers in a bar were discussing whether making love was work or pleasure. The youngest said it was definitely pleasure. The 50 year old said well, sometimes pleasure, sometimes work. The 70 year old said he was afraid that now he found it mainly work. Trying to settle the friendly argument, they turned to a grieve having an evening pint and asked for his opinion.

"Definitely pleasure," he said. "If it was work you'd get me to do it for you."

Fordyce Maxwell, formerly Scotsman

David Leggat was conducting a roup. Among the items were some household items, including a parrot in a cage. One old farmer took a shine to it and started the bidding at a tenner. Quickly a better bid of £12 followed. The old farmer dug in as the bids climbed, but looked as he was beaten at £40. One last bid of £42 got it for him. He then asked David ruefully, "I hope it can speak at that price."

"Speak?" said David. "Who do you think was bidding against you?"

Peter Stewart, Urquhart

NINE

Mary was feeling grumpy because Wullie had not been 'active in the bedroom department' for ages. The two of them were at the Highland Show looking at bulls. Mary said, "This bull has sired 100 calves. That's 100 times Wullie that he's been active; unlike some."

Wullie growled under his breath. "Ooh," said Mary, "This bull has sired 150 calves. That's 150 times.... So there is nothing wrong with his libido; unlike some."

Wullie growled again.

Approaching a massive beast, Mary said, "Now look at him. He has sired 200 calves. That's 200 times he's been active."

Wullie was heard to mutter, "Aye but not all with the same old cow."
Bob Noble, formerly Duns and Borders NFU

There was the old shepherd who complained that the recent storm had been so strong that "even the crows were walking."
Peter Small, Falfield

The agricultural salesman was on his rounds when he saw a crowd of people gathering outside a farmhouse.

It was a cold November afternoon, so he stopped and asked one of the throng why such a large crowd had gathered there.

The reply came, "Old Smith's donkey kicked his mother-in-law and she died."

"Well," replied the salesman, "The old lady must have had a lot of friends."

"Not at all," was the response. "We all just want to buy the donkey."
Anon

The farmer went to market and after having his lunch at the nearby hotel, the waitress asked how he enjoyed his meal.

"Well," he said, "I felt the steak was a bit over cooked."

"Next time you should ask for a bloody steak," she advised.

The following week he went back and this time he was accompanied by his small son. When the waitress asked for his order he answered, "I'll have a bloody steak."

His son then piped up, "That's the way to talk faither. Bring me a f....ing pie!"

Martha and Ramsay Sykes, Coylton

Jimmy Nicol was a well-known farmer at Clashfarquhar, near Aberdeen. He was a prominent breeder of Aberdeen-Angus, with a niche market for heifers of the Luxury family in America, but he really made his money on the stock market, learning his investment skills from his officers during the First World War where his harrowing job was taking bodies back from the front. In the 1960s, he bought the Bay Hotel, the biggest hotel in Stonehaven, which he presented to the Church of Scotland for an old folk's home (Clashfarquhar House which still exists) and lived there himself until he died at the age of 99.

On a trip to New Zealand, he wanted to meet the Governor, Sir Bernard Fergusson, and asked the porter at the hotel how he should go about it. Jimmy was a bachelor and not exactly the epitome of sartorial elegance. The porter drew himself up to his full height and, looking down his nose at wee Jimmy who was about 4ft 11in, said, "You can't just go and see the Governor you know without an appointment." The next thing the porter saw was the Governor's Rolls Royce drawing up outside the hotel and Jimmy getting on board. When he came back, the porter was all over him: "Did you serve under Sir Bernard during the war?" he asked. Jimmy never broke his stride: "No," he said as he marched on. "He served under me!"

It turned out that Sir Bernard and Jimmy had indeed served in the Gordon Highlanders together. Sir Bernard had joined as a private while Jimmy by this time, had risen to the dizzy heights of corporal!

Eddie Gillanders, Farm North East

Bob Urquhart, the revered agricultural editor of the Scotsman in the 1950s and 1960s and the man credited with making the Royal Highland and Agricultural Society of Scotland aware that Ingliston Estate was on the market, had rather a good war, reaching the rank of Squadron Leader in the RAF. Often, post-war, he would spend week-ends with Lord Lovat at Beaufort Castle. He was not averse to boasting about his wartime exploits and his connections with the aristocracy. But he was soon brought down to earth by Alex Munro, the agricultural editor of the Press and Journal, who had given Bob, who had been working in a draper's shop in Banff, his first job in journalism while he was editor of the Banffshire Journal. "Aye, Bob," he would say. "If it wisnae for me, you'd still be sellin' hunkies in Banff.."

Eddie Gillanders, Farm North East

A well known Orcadian farmer was also a part time taxi driver. One day he was sitting in his taxi waiting at Kirkwall Airport for a fare. A smartly dressed gentleman just off the plane approached and asked if he knew where xxx farm was. "Sure I do," replied the taxi driver not revealing it was his own farm. As they drove along towards it, the taxi driver casually asked his passenger what brought him to Orkney. "I'm a VAT inspector," replied the passenger.

Still not revealing his identity, the taxi driver/farmer drove up to his own farmhouse door. "Do you want me to wait?" he asked his customer. "That would be good," he replied as he knocked on the door of the empty house. After a few minutes of fruitless knocking, he walked round the steading but found no one. "I suppose you had better take me back," he instructed the driver.

Again as they drove back, the driver asked as casually as he could, "Where to?" "To the airport," was the response and he did not hear the sigh of relief from his driver.

Anon

The vet was in his surgery when the phone rang. It was a bad line but he thought he heard the farmer complaining he had a calf with colic.

"I am busy just now. Just give it two large spoonfuls of cod liver oil and I will look round later," said the vet.

True to his word, he called on the farm and asked to see the sickly calf.

"It wisnae a calf, it was a cat," said the farmer.

"Where is the cat then?" asked the vet.

"He is out the back with three other cats," came the reply. "One is digging holes, one is filling them in and the third is looking for fresh ground.

Peter Small, Falfield

In 1946 my father, Gordon Porter, went to interview a cattleman who was working for Col Forbes at Balglassie.

The man, Joe Paton, had been given a good reference.

As was the custom at that time, the Grieve accompanied him.

It was dark when they arrived at the cottage. Joe's wife showed them into a poorly lit room. Father said he could just make out the man sitting in the corner but he could not persuade him to leave his seat so he could confirm his stature. After some talk, my father decided to fee Joe but he was keen to see him off his backside so he held out his arles*. Thereupon Joe slipped off his chair which had been built up with cushions. He was only five foot tall with a hunch back.

After their departure, the grieve burst out laughing and commented, "I dinna think that lad will last long at the Scryne." Well Joe died 50 years to the month after he arrived. He scarcely missed a day's work. He was quite cantankerous, swore a lot, especially if someone took his besom or graip, but he was such a character that everyone liked him.

He was a very good cattleman and was very upset if he lost a beast or calf.

*arles were paid to seal a deal with a new employee

Willie Porter, West Scryne

It was a bitterly cold morning and the two Aberdeenshire loons were happy they had a warming job; spreading out the heaps of dung left by the carts emptying the cattle courts. As they worked their way across the frosty fields they welcomed the heat from the warm dung.

Then lying in the frozen stubble they came across a little bird. They thought it was dead but they picked it up and carefully placed it in the warm dung.

Slowly the little bird regained the will to live and it stuck its head out of the dung and started to sing. Hearing the bird song, a hawk swooped down and had the bird for lunch.

The lessons from this tale are;

It is not always your enemies that drop you in it.

It is not always your friends that get you out of it

And if you are up to your neck in sh*t, keep your mouth shut.

Anon

In the seventies, the company Peebles Bros was taken over by Ross Produce. During the transition period from one company to another, David Peebles had two phone lines, one number for each company. One Friday afternoon, a farmer called looking for a price for 20 tonnes of Maris Piper, so David quoted him £100 per tonne. A few minutes later the other phone rang and David recognised the voice as the same farmer he had just quoted. Cannily, David quoted him £110 per tonne and the farmer complained that he could buy them for £100 per tonne elsewhere. "You'd better go and buy them then," said David, and the farmer agreed to do just that. Sure enough the other phone rang again and David sold him the load at £100 per tonne. The happy farmer mentioned that some other fool tried to charge him £10 per tonne extra and David agreed that that guy must be a right pillock.

Peter Peebles, Greenvale

The first time I judged sheep was at a wet and windy Fife Show at Balcormo. There were a lot of Border Leicesters entered, including ones from Hugh Stewart of Struthers and his brother John of Kininmonth.

I put John's ewe champion that day and Hugh's was well down the cut. On walking back to the beer tent with Hugh I asked him, "How do you think I judged, Mr Stewart?"

Without breaking a stride, he replied, "Ye ken nothing about sheep laddie."

I never asked anyone again how I had judged.

Johnny Morison, QMS Assessor

The question auctioneers are often asked is "what is the most unusual lot you have ever auctioned?"

One of the most unusual lots I had to sell was a Harley Street vasectomy which came up for auction at Save the Rhino charity function near Cheltenham. The lot caused quite a stir and amusement, however bidders were shy and it sold for what I was told was around half its value. It could be said it was "quite a snip."

David Leggat, United Auctions

Many years ago, before decimalisation, a bachelor farmer was getting ready for church - he was running late so he told his maid to go to the money box in the pantry, get two pennies and put them in his waistcoat pocket. Come offering time in church, as he dropped the money in the plate, he noticed it was two half crowns but he didn't want to ask for them back.

However when the plate came round the next Sunday, he looked up at the collector and said, "Season ticket!!"

Ronnie McLauchlan, Ballachulish

Feeling there was a need to diversify and generate more income, a farmer decided to rear budgies. When taking his first load to the market the driver of a car following him noticed that every few hundred yards the farmer stuck his hand out the window and thumped the side of his van. This went on for a good few miles until the farmer turned into a petrol station. Intrigued the car driver followed him and asked why he kept thumping the side of his van.

"Oh," said the farmer as he thumped the side of the van again. "I've a terrible problem. This is a five hundredweight van and I've got ten hundredweight of budgies in the back. If I don't keep the b*ggers flying they'll burst the springs."

Alistair Donaldson, formerly Meat and Livestock Commission

A past president of Marnoch Branch, John farmed a really boggy, wet farm. When the factor, visiting on a rent review, suggested a rent of fifteen shillings, John queried if that would be per gallon or per acre.

Alan Meldrum, formerly NFUS Banff

During the war thousands of troops were stationed in Orkney. At that time on smaller farms many of the cattle were tethered on the grass. One soldier writing home explained that he was in Orkney where it was "so windy that farmers had to tie their cattle to the ground with rope".

George Burgher, formerly NFUS Orkney & Shetland

Bill Rennie acted as an expert witness at Stonehaven Sheriff Court in a dispute between two Aberdeenshire farmers over the quality of spring barley that one had bought from the other. The whole case was conducted in the Doric and was presided over by a sheriff with a well developed sense of humour.

The purchaser found that the seed barley produced a poor stand and claimed that it was not fit for purpose. The Sheriff asked the claimant how he had come to buy the seed. Had he seen it before he bought it?

"Oh aye," he responded. "I hae visited my neeboor's ferm and saw the barley for ma sell. He had it in a railway carriage."

"Do you mean a goods wagon or was it in fact a railway carriage?" There followed a discussion on the type of container, all in the Doric. To bring the discussion to a close the sheriff asked was it first or second class?

"Ah dinna rightly recall," said the buyer. Then after a period of silence he offered, "But, man, it wis first class for holdin seed barley."

The sheriff found in favour of the claimant.

Bill Rennie, British Society for Plant Pathology

Sandy Inverarity told the story at the NFU AGM at Rothesay in 1971 of the two local farmers who saw a dark object in the sea.

One said "What's that?"

The other said, "It's a board".

"Is it moving forward?"

"Yes," came the reply.

"Well it's certainly not the Scottish Milk Marketing Board!"

George Burgher, formerly Orkney & Shetland NFUS secretary

Frank Roger was a remarkable man. In the early 1960s, his son Bill gave me a holiday house in Boarhills, so my family spent the summer there and I stayed at weekends. If Frank Roger said he would pick you up at 7am for a run round his stock – cattle or sheep – he would be at your door at 7am and away we would go. If we were going up the main road, past the church, Frank would have the car still in 1st gear – roaring like an aeroplane on a runway – then he would take both hands from the steering wheel and with both hands would let the gear slide from 1st to 4th in one movement. The first time I was nearly through the windscreen but after that you were ready as the car jerked forward until it settled down. One day Frank asked Bill to change his car and when Bill went to the garage, the salesman asked what state the car was in. Bill told him that 2nd and 3rd gears were like new as they had never been used.

John Chapman, James Chapman, (Butchers Ltd)

After a busy day showing pedigree cattle at the Highland show a Scottish farming couple sat down in the herdsman's restaurant to have a bite to eat and a few drinks.

They were joined by a Texan Rancher and his wife, who became louder and louder, the more they drank. The Texan proclaimed that it took him 3 days to drive in his pick-up to the furthest side of his ranch and his wife complained that the Scottish steaks served up were so small compared to those in America. The Scottish farmer just sat there biting his lip in the off chance the Rancher might buy one of his bulls.

However his wife, fuelled by alcohol, could not contain herself any longer and blurted out, "My man used to hae a truck like that but wis forced to scrap it and in Scotland steaks are usually served up in portions tae fit yer moo."

Graham Bruce, Ringlink

The old man was living alone on his farm and his only son John was in prison. He wrote to his son and explained that as he was no longer fit to dig his garden, he was unable to plant his tatties. In the next post he received a letter: "Dear Dad. Do not dig the garden as I buried the bodies there. Love, John."

Soon afterwards a squad of policemen arrived and dug up the whole garden. Later in the week the old farmer received another letter: "Dear Dad. You can now plant your tatties. That is the best that I could do in the circumstances. Love, John."

George Burgher, formerly Orkney & Shetland NFUS secretary

The well-known journalist and author, Jack Webster, whose father was the renowned auctioneer at Maud mart, tells this story in his autobiography. Everyone had their own story about how severe the famous 1953 gale was and how badly they had been affected. But, Jack says, nobody could cap his father's story.

"Michty, there wis sic a gale, fin the dog opened his moo tae bark he farted!"

Eddie Gillanders, Farm North East

Recognising faces and putting names to them is an essential quality for an auctioneer. Forgetting a face can be very embarrassing.

At a large farm sale at Bankhead, Forteviot I was selling the implements. As we were nearing the end of the sale I was aware of a tall individual in a donkey jacket, Argyll wellies and torn denims. He was bidding on items but not successfully. I knew that I should know the face but could not remember from where.

He was eventually successful and bought a lot. I uttered the famous line "I am sorry sir, I should know your name".

He shouted out, "You should know my name, I'm your minister!"

The Reverend Colin Williamson dined out on this incident for years.

David Leggat, United Auctions

TEN

An inspector visited a village school and asked one small boy, a shepherd's son, a question: "If there are 53 sheep in a field and 11 get out through a hole in the fence, how many are left?"

"None," the boy replied immediately.

The inspector turned to the teacher. "This boy obviously knows very little about arithmetic."

"And you," said the boy, "know b*gger all about sheep."

Fordyce Maxwell, formerly Scotsman

In Orkney in the late 1800s, if pilot whales were spotted, every boat was manned and every effort was made to drive the whales ashore so that the blubber could be sold to provide much needed oil. John, a crofter from Westray, lost his wife one night and at daybreak there was a cry of "Whales in the Bay". He immediately went to the undertaker and asked him to make a coffin for her. This not only meant that the undertaker and his assistants would be unable to share the spoils when the whales were captured, but it also meant that John could take part in the whale hunt and get his share. A large number of whales were slain and a neighbouring proprietor was asked to go and divide the spoils. The laird who had heard of John's sad loss was amazed to find John excitedly taking part in the whale slaughter and remonstrated with him about his presence at such a time. John replied, "Well you see, laird, I could na afford to lose both wife and whales in the same day."

George Burgher, formerly Orkney & Shetland NFUS secretary

The Garden Festival held in Glasgow introduced loads of city children to farming. There was a milking demonstration with clear plastic pipes showing the milk travelling through them. Scottish Farm Minister, Lord Sanderson asked two young boys watching this if they had learned anything.

One laddie replied, "Ah now ken how they get the milk into the coo."

Hilary Barker, Farm Organiser at the Festival, Callander

When I was still at school, he used to enjoy the visits of the vets, as they were full of tales and they were also the best educated visitors to the farm.

One day the vet was working on a cow and chuckling to himself. When I asked what was funny, he told me he had been in at another farm and was struggling to hold the bottle of calcium in his right hand while also working the needle with his left.

The old farmer offered to help even though he was steadying the beast.

"It's ok," said the vet, "I'm ambidextrous."

"Oh," said the farmer. "I always thought there was something funny about you."

Peter Stewart, Urquhart

At a Union branch meeting in the West of Scotland, the chairman was looking to fill the committee places. All went well until he came to the Land Use and Environment post. He got no volunteers, and sought to persuade the unfortunate who had already accepted the Legal and Technical remit. The clearly unwilling target asked what was involved. The bemused chairman looked around for guidance, and of course got none. Then inspiration struck, and he said, "Slurry! Slurry will be covered by this committee."

The victim pondered for a moment, then replied in a broad west coast accent that, although he was undoubtedly an expert in slurry, with his education the legal position fitted him better.

Peter Stewart, Urquhart

During my term as Chairman of Scotrail we had an annual visit from the Minister of Transport from London. This was an important date for us in Scotrail because it was the occasion for us to make our annual request for support in the form of subsidy for maintaining the services on our 'rural' routes to places like Oban, Mallaig, Thurso and Kyle of Lochalsh.

On this occasion the Minister was flying up to Inverness so I decided to take him down to Kyle in the Scotrail Saloon. If ever a line needed support, it was the line from Inverness to Kyle!

Whilst waiting for the Minister to arrive I got the crew together to explain the importance of the journey and the need to suitably impress the Minister. Our guard for the day was from Kyle. He was a real character by the name of MacLeod and I briefed him accordingly.

In due course the Minister arrived and we set off for Kyle. All went well until somewhere between Auchnasheen and Auchnashelloch the train stopped in the middle of nowhere. I wasn't overly concerned as I was hopeful that our guard MacLeod would be along with a suitable explanation, although I could see the Minister was wondering why we had stopped.

Eventually, MacLeod appeared and said in his lilting West Highland accent – much to my embarrassment – that he was sorry for the delay but there was "a sheep on the line".

The Minister, knowing my agricultural background, was obviously highly amused. Eventually the train got under way and conversation resumed again.

You can imagine my frustration however when we stopped again a little way down the line. This time the Minister, sensing my growing concern, was hardly able to conceal his amusement. I was about to summon Macleod again when he appeared at the saloon door. Before either he or I could say anything however, the Minister who did have a sense of humour, said, "Well guard, I suppose that's another sheep on the line?" Before I could think of how to follow the Minister's remark, MacLeod who had summed up the situation perfectly and with a twinkle in his eye said "Not at all sir. Not another sheep on the line at all. It was the same sheep."

The next day I made MacLeod station master at Inverness.

John Cameron, Balbuthie

The pea vining season had come to an end in Fife and to celebrate, the farmers held a dance. At the end of the evening, the chairman generously invited the assembled crowd back to his house for coffee. One couple was none too sure of exactly where the farm was located but eventually saw this house with an outside light on.

'That is it,' they decided but within yards of turning off the public road, their four wheel drive was put severely to the test, bumping over what seemed like boulders. Thankfully, the rough section soon passed and the next section up to the house was smooth and dead level.

They saw the host at the door but his welcome was ever so slightly frosty. "Do you realise you have just driven up over my rockery and across my lawn?" he asked

Anon

One morning a semi-retired farmer finished breakfast and went from the kitchen through the sun parlour and sat down. It was a beautiful sunny morning and as he sat there admiring the cattle grazing in the field and thinking what a lovely day it was going to be his wife came and sat down beside him. "Well," she said, "what are you going to do today?"

There was a slight pause and then he answered, "I'm not going to do anything. I'm going to do nothing" - but she said "You did nothing yesterday."

"Yes" he said, "but I didn't finish it."

Ronnie McLauchlan, Tulliemet

Another auction, another ring and the bidding was sticky to say the least. The auctioneer bent down to the consigner asking for advice and help. "She could be in calf but I am not sure" did not exactly push the bidding up.

Anon

It is not unusual for cereal growers to become itchy and impatient when harvest is on the horizon and this particular farmer in the East Neuk of Fife was no exception. He deemed his crop was ripe and after instructing the student on the farm to follow him with the grain trailer he fired up his old combine and headed off down to the first field. He was only halfway round the first bout when he noticed a wisp of smoke coming from the combine dashboard. Sensing there was a problem, he shouted to the student to rush back to the farm steading to get a fire extinguisher. Off the lad went with the trailer bouncing along behind him. The smoke from behind the dashboard grew stronger and soon there were flames lipping round the switches. There was still no sign of the boy returning as the farmer in desperation tried to smother the flames with his old bonnet. This amateur fire fighting was useless. The combine cab was soon ablaze and still there was no sign of the boy returning with the extinguisher. The farmer abandoned his combine with the fire spreading to all parts. Only after it was totally ablaze did the boy appear and any rescue bid was far too late.

"Where have you been?" the farmer asked angrily.

"There was a man in at the farm when I got back. He wanted to buy a bag of potatoes so I sold him one. Here is your £2."

Anon

The life of a farming reporter covering the many agricultural shows means he or she always has to have their notebook at the ready to get the comments of the victorious as well as the breeding of the champions; although the sceptical reporter knows this latter information can vary from show to show. At one show, I spied Willie, who was always in among the silverware. I asked if he had any success. As he slowly answered, "I've wan…" I reached for my notebook. He paused and then, when he saw I was ready to take down the breeding and previous successes of the champion, Willie continued, "I've wan b*gger all."

Andrew Arbuckle

A local bachelor farmer was in court on charges of "being a nuisance to a major firm."

The firm claimed they continually had to write to him with the following message.

"Dear Mr Smith. Please do not keep writing to our firm. SCREWFIX is not a dating agency."

Gavin Hill, SAC Consulting

A farmer went to his bank manager and said he would like to withdraw £100 as he was going to Smithfield and his wife would be doing some shopping in London at the same time. He went back the following week and said his wife could no longer go with him so could he please have another £200.

Alistair Donaldson, formerly Meat and Livestock Commission

A farming couple were out having a bar meal. When the waiter approached the table and put down the food, the lady slipped down and hid under the table.

"Excuse me Sir, I think your wife is under the table," said the waiter.

"No, she isn't," replied the farmer, "She has just walked in the door".

Robin Niven, Loch Leven's Larder

In the days of the Milk Marketing Board in Orkney, not only did they operate the local creamery but they also ran the artificial insemination service. One of the local SWRI Branches had planned that their local outing would be a visit to the creamery. The branch secretary telephoned to arrange the visit and after some delay got through and asked, "Do you think you could handle a party of 25 women?" After a lengthy pause a voice queried, "Do you realise that you are talking to the AI man?"

George Burgher, formerly Orkney & Shetland NFUS secretary

Back in the days where the Courier not only carried all the show results but also who the judges were, I used the show catalogue for the information. The result was one Monday morning after a show, I received a phone call from an irate exhibitor. "I just want you to know the judge you have in the paper died a week ago but even if he was dead he could have done a better job than the man who took his place." Feeling better after his outburst, he then put the phone down.

Andrew Arbuckle

A crofter won £3 million on the Lottery. He and his wife decided to put it all in the bank but the following winter the pair of them decided to spend some of the cash on a patio round the house to stop the muck being brought inside. The patio was built and one day when they were both sitting having their tea, the talk turned to the toilet at the bottom of the garden. It was agreed they would spend some more of the prize money on an inside toilet. The plumbers were brought in and a new toilet was built inside.

Sometime later, a visitor came to the croft. "I am from Camelot. We are doing a survey on how the prize money has been spent. Has it made a difference to your life?"

"Aye, aye," replied the crofter. "Before we won, we used to eat in the house and sh*t in the garden. Now we eat in the garden and sh*t in the house."

Willie McLaren Snr, Netherton

Bob Urquhart claimed the most beautiful sight in Scotland could be viewed from the top of Ben Rinnes. "You can see 60 distilleries and a' workin'," he would say.

Eddie Gillanders, Farm North East

Anyone who has ever run a berry squad will know of the need for speed. A gang of pickers has no patience when the berry crop is "hinging" and they will suffer no delay. One day back in the 1970's we had started the day's picking when I realised that the rasps weren't good enough for picking into baskets and we would have to change to pulp.

This of course meant changing the scales and issuing everyone with big plastic buckets and "luggies" (small pails) for the picker to tie round their waists. I was busily setting up the scales. There was no time to muck around and I shouted over my shoulder to the student who was helping me to tare a bucket so that I had an empty weight to work on. "What?" he asked. "Tare a bucket and be quick!" I shouted back. When I turned round I found him blue in the face with exertion trying to tear a thick plastic bucket in half without really knowing what he was supposed to be doing.

It may be 45 years on but my bet is that the hapless student - now a prominent Dundee businessman - still remembers the difference between "tare" and "tear". I explained it to him very clearly at the time!

Ewan Pate, Courier

The farmer was admiring his tidy farm when a tourist drew up. "That is a real neat place you have there. Praise to you and the Lord for your efforts." The proud farmer was not willing to share the adulation. "You should have seen it when he had it on his own."

Anon

McTavish was not the fastest individual on the planet and his farmer friends would often mock him for his very slow pace in doing anything. One night as he returned to the farmhouse for tea and was about to take his boots off at the front porch, he turned and crushed a snail into the ground.

"Why on earth did you do that?" demanded his wife. He replied, "It was getting on my nerves. It's been following me about all day."

Judith O'Leary, O'Leary PR, Dunfermline

This farmer had the contract to supply beef to Perth prison and when the contract was up for renewal he was interviewed by members of the prison board

"Mr.*********, we have had a few complaints recently about the beef being very tough."

He replied, "Aweel, the lads in here'll hae plenty time tae chow it."

Louis Flood, photographer, Perth

A minister visits the farm one day and notices the farmer is wearing an earring.

The man knows the minister is a conservative fellow, and is curious about his sudden change in fashion sense.

The minister walks up and says, "I didn't know you were into wearing earrings."

"Don't worry, it's only an earring," the farmer replies sheepishly.

The minister falls silent for a few minutes, but then his curiosity prods him to ask, "So, how long have you been wearing one?"

"Ever since my wife found it in the back of my old Land Rover."

Bruce Jobson, Morpeth

A farmer complained, "I have only today received the subsidy for manure which was passed by a Department Official six months ago."

George Burgher, formerly Orkney & Shetland NFUS secretary

ELEVEN

The small lighthouse island of Copinsay in Orkney has a 200 foot high cliff which has many ledges on which birds such as guillemots nest. In the latter part of the 19th century the wild birds' eggs were collected for sale annually by daring cragsmen climbing down the cliff face with stout ropes tied around their waists. Children of the family who lived on the island and farmed it imitated the older men by doing some rock climbing on lower, smaller cliffs using knotted binder twine. A lighthouse keeper who saw them asked, "What if the binder twine breaks?"

"Oh, there's plenty more in the barn," was the quick reply.

George Burgher, formerly Orkney & Shetland NFUS secretary

A well known sheep dog trialist came over from his Arran base to compete in a top event. It was a successful foray and after being presented with the cup, he went off to celebrate before boarding the ferry home. Before entering the hostelry, he tied his dog up on the pier. Emerging later, filled with his success and strong drink, he completely forgot about his prize winning pooch. Thankfully the ferrymen put the abandoned dog on the next boat.

This forgetfulness, aggravated by alcohol, is not unique as one Fife farmer managed to go home without his prize winning lamb after celebrating his success. This necessitated a return to the showfield next morning to pick up the abandoned champion.

Anon

A farmer's son, slowly making his way in the world outside the farm, was talking to an older relative at a funeral. When asked how things were going, the young lad rattled off a list of grumbles and grievances about his office job.

To which the older farmer said, "Well, if ye enjoy yer work, ye're probably no daein' it right!"

John D Arbuckle, North Berwick

John McLaren, Wester Keillour was asked to be the quiz master at a Women's Rural meeting. The competition at those events was always fierce and the answers came flying back. However, he had everyone stumped when he asked the question, "How do you make cheuch pastry?" There were, as years of competitions could testify, many top class cooks in the meeting but this question had them beat. At least until one lady asked if she could see the question card.

"It's choux pastry, he wants to know about," she announced in a superior manner.

Anon

Our long serving cattleman Dave Boath was one of those guys who performed a range .of tasks every year with unfailing good humour. One of these jobs was manning the back of the tattie dresser and because he was a big strong man he was always on the seed side. As he was getting a little older, I thought he could do with a little help manhandling the 50 kilo (hundredweight) bags on to the pallets and so decided to buy a hydraulic bag lifter. This was a simple enough machine like a mini-fork lift with a mast and platform. The idea was that as soon as the bag was placed on the ground level platform an electronic switch would be triggered and the bag would rise effortlessly up to shoulder height. All the operator had to do was flick the bag on to his shoulder and thence on to the waiting pallet. The platform would then travel unbidden back down the mast ready to receive the next bag.

On the great day that the machine arrived everyone was gathered round to see the first bag elevated skyward. Dave placed the bag on the platform, up it went and he grabbed it in copybook fashion. The only problem was that he forgot to take the obligatory half step backwards allowing the descending platform to rather neatly hook itself into the gaping trouser pocket of Dave's voluminous corduroys. In an instant- much to the delight of the on-looking "tattie wifies"- his breeks were round his ankles. Of course he could do nothing about it because he still had a 50 kilo bag of tatties on his shoulder.

Thank goodness for his natty flanellette pantaloons. Only they saved him from the ultimate exposure!. After that he always smartly took the wee step backwards but the wifies kept an eagle eye open in case of any repetition.

Ewan Pate, Courier

The minister was going round his parish and enjoying hospitality as he went. At one farm, he was offered a whisky with the farmer announcing proudly, he was drinking 15 year old Highland Park. The minister raised his glass and commented, "My it's awful wee for its age."

Willie McLaren Snr, Netherton

I was having a drink at the Perth bull sales with Captain Ben Coutts when he was secretary of the Aberdeen-Angus Cattle Society. I made a move to take out my wallet and pay. "It's ok," said Ben. "I'll do the paying - you can do the fumbling!"

Eddie Gillanders, Farm North East

One night drinking in the local with my drouthy cronies in Auchtermuchty I noticed a new chap in the corner of the bar. On introducing myself I found he was a newcomer and he was planning to open a restaurant in the town. After a while the conversation turned a bit sour shall we say. The next thing I knew I had been Karate chopped and was writhing about on the floor in agony.

"What the h*ll was that all about? "I asked.

"Haa so that was a one two three Karate chop," as he left

Next day while passing by the pub I saw my new 'friend' making his way to the pub so I turned the tractor round and headed back.

On entering, I saw him standing at the bar. I removed a long metal object from my piece bag and give him a sharp crack between the legs with it. "Oh oh oh. So what was that all about?" he asked in agony.

"That my friend was a 135 top link. "

Murdo Fraser, Pitcairlie

A couple were out in one of the sheds on their farm one evening. It dawned on the wife that the following week was their golden wedding anniversary. She turned to her husband and pointed out the significance of next week. She added the thought that they might have a celebratory meal to mark the occasion and suggested that they kill a lamb. After thinking for a moment, the husband replied, "Och Jean, it's not really fair to hold a wee lamb responsible for something that happened almost 50 years ago."

Liam McArthur MSP

Two guys in the foreign legion are walking across the desert in the midday sun when one said to the other, "It's the date of the Fife agricultural show today."

The other replied, "Well they've got a good day for it."

Rosemary Walker, Playfair Walker PR

Geordie was a bachelor farmer who eked a living in the hill country of Northumberland. His ageing aunt kept house and cooked his meals. One March morning after checking the stock, he returned to the farmhouse for breakfast as usual. The old lady was sitting at the range apparently in the process of making the porridge. Geordie approached her only to find that she had passed away. She sat rigid, the porridge spoon in her hand. Geordie was shocked. A few days later he was reciting the story to another relative. "And what did you do?" asked the concerned cousin. "I had corn flakes," he confided.

Bill Howatson, formerly Press & Journal

Years ago I was privileged to have wheat variety trials on a superbly managed farm in Angus. The seed for these trials came from breeders or their agents so we had no control over the cleanliness of the seed. That meant that we had to be on the lookout for wild oats, not just because it would be a dreadful way of rewarding those good enough to supply us with a trial site, but also because if we would contaminate our combine and thus spread wild oats to other sites. I was spotted by the farmer walking the plots and was quizzed about what I was doing. So I told him I was checking for wild-oats to which he replied, I hope in jest, "If you leave any I'll shoot you."

Next year we were chatting and I spotted roguers in his fields so I challenged him and reminded him about his threat to shoot me if he saw any wild oats.

He replied, "Aye, but that was after my fields had been rogued."

David Cranstoun, retired SAC advisor

Not long after I was elected as a councillor in Fife, I was asked to judge the Pets' Parade at the local gala. I was faced with everything from big dogs to stick insects and, like most interbreed judges, was left in a bit of a quandary. On the basis of if you are going to make a mess of it do it quickly, I soon picked out a rather fat rabbit. As I left the ring, my judging stint completed, I heard an old farmer comment, "That is one vote he has gained and twelve he has lost."

I never judged again.

Andrew Arbuckle

Even in the days when it was stacked in coles making hay was a catchy business. One wet year, Frank Roger, Kenly Green, took advantage of a rare dry day to make his coles. His neighbour, whose hayfield was just over the dyke, shook his head and declared Roger was being too impatient, the hay was not ready.

Two weeks of rain followed during which time the neighbour's hay still lying in the bout turned black. The first dry day came and saw a salvage job started. Frank looked over the dyke and drily remarked, "It will be about ready now."

Jo Roger, St Andrews

A roup at Bannaty farm, Milnathort in the 1990s attracted both father and son Stevenson from Ballingry farm. During the sale they went their separate ways. The auctioneer came to a pile of drainage pipes and started the bidding which went upwards above the expected price. Suddenly he stopped and pointed his gavel at the father and said, "You're bidding," and then turned to the son and pointed out, "You're also bidding." Before either party could retract their bid, he banged the gavel down, "Sold."

George Lawrie, Balado

Vagrants in the olden days, on the whole, hadn't such a bad existence. It wasn't uncommon, two hundred years ago for lairds and farmers to entertain beggars with great kindness, giving them supper and breakfast as well as a bed in one of the outhouses. Those of them who were crippled or blind were hospitably treated wherever they went, but at the same time they were a burden on the charitable. In addition to giving them food and shelter, the families relieving them had to carry or lead them to the next house.

Some of the cripples had to be carried from place-to-place and door-to-door in boxes or hand-barrows. In course of time they almost looked upon the public as their bound servants, demanding such acts of kindness and charity as a right.

One escapade with a cripple in Crawick Valley, near Sanquhar saw him arrive in his hand-barrow at Carco Mains, where he was treated to a substantial dinner by the kind-hearted farmer who afterwards entrusted two servant lads to convey him to Knockenstob, the next farmhouse.

Taking a shortcut through the fields, when the lads were about half way through their task they were alarmed by the bellowing of a bull. On looking round they saw an angry animal about to charge at them and as the bull began to make for them, they dropped the beggar man and ran with all their might for a friendly dyke. Imagine their surprise when the supposed cripple also took to his heels.

More fleet of foot than those who had carried him, he cleared the dyke in a bound and, not stopping to look behind him, was soon out of sight. He didn't return for his hand-barrow, nor was he ever seen on Crawick banks again!

Rog Wood, Herald

Before he met and married Rosemary who provided him with a readymade and happy family, Sandy Braid was a long term bachelor. For decades he went to dances all over Scotland. Late in his bachelor days he was dancing with this young girl. She asked him his name and when he told her, she gave the ego crushing reply. "Oh, my mum used to go out with you."

Anon

Being Show Secretary you were also the licence holder for the bar at the event with closing time one in the morning. The venue was always at the extreme end of the island, with a single track road down to the village hall. The tradition was that the Secretary after a hard day at the Show would also be committed to entertain business customers for a meal that night. After that he then went down to the dance to ensure the bar run by the Show committee was closed down at the agreed legal time. The police brought in from the mainland always visited to ensure the terms of the licence were enforced and then they were expected to go back up the fifteen mile single track road and never be seen again that night. After all the Chief Inspector from Glasgow was there on holiday as was his tradition every year. As was also traditional every year, once the bar had been closed and confirmed by police they would go on their way. Then the bar re-opened until three in the morning, or as long as the band could be persuaded to play.

This particular year the Secretary arrived at 10.55pm and was greeted by Ian in charge of the bar. "We are running out of beer John. We will need to go down to Sandy at the local shop and wake him up to get more."

The Secretary then suggested, "Let's just wait until the police have seen us and closed the bar down, then we will get your van and go down to Sandy."

As was expected the police duly arrived. They saw the bar closed on time and then left. Ian grabbed the van, drove down to Sandy and started loading the van with cases of beer. What was not expected was the police car doing an extra circuit of the village. At the last minute Ian saw the light of the patrol car and quickly started to unload the van. In a load voice he said, "Bad night Sandy. Did not sell half the beer we expected."

Once the patrol car was out of sight, they started loading the beer back into the van. After all, they did not want to disappoint the Chief Inspector.

John Cruickshanks, Kelso and RBS

My father Robert Holmes, formerly of Pilmuir farm used to say that the rattle of the Dickie hay turner would bring on the rain.

Heather Holmes, Edinburgh

A few years ago Jock set out from the Isle of Lewis to buy his ram at Kelso. It was a long journey and he and his friend Tam took the evening ferry from Stornoway across to Ullapool and made the long journey south in his old jeep, pulling a small trailer for the return journey.

They arrived in Kelso early on the Friday morning with plenty of time to view the fine selection of rams on offer and were soon in action bidding on the earlier lots into the ring.

By lunch time they had their selection purchased and decided they had time for a 'wee dram' before heading back to Ullapool to catch the late ferry back to Lewis.

Well replenished with food and drink and after a brief 'discussion' on who was driving, off they set on the long journey north. They duly arrived at the ferry where the ticket inspector asked where they had been and what they had been up to, to which they proudly replied that they had been to 'the biggest ram sale in the world to buy a ram' and furthermore 'would he like to see it?'

They climbed down from the jeep, went round to the trailer and - you've guessed it - they had forgotten to load the ram!

Hilary Jackson, Agritiser

The farmer had problems with his heart so he went to his doctor. After examining him, the doctor advised him to have a glass of red wine before he went to bed and come back in three months. He did as he was told and when asked how he felt by the doctor, he declared he had never felt better. "I went to bed ten times yesterday," he admitted.

Willie McLaren Snr, Netherton

A farmer's wife told a friend she was going to Venice. "Oh, lovely," said the friend, "Is it a romantic trip?"

"No," the farmer's wife said, "I'm going with my husband."

Fordyce Maxwell

The late Matt Mundell was writing up the results of a show when someone in the office asked him what he was doing. "Just typing out all the second prize winners," was his laconic response.

"Should that not be the champions and first prize winners?" was the obvious question.

"Because every one of the farmers round the judging ring was heard telling their neighbours after the judge chose his champion, 'I've a better one than that at home.'"

Bill Howatson, formerly Press & Journal

The new employee had just started work on the farm, when the farmer sent him to open up a field of corn. To make sure he did a good job, the farmer sharpened the scythe. Handing it over, he claimed, "There you are, that scythe is so sharp now it will go itself."

The farmer went off to the market and when he came home he went to see how his new employee had got on. There he found the so called worker sitting up against a tree with no work done.

Enraged the farmer asked, "What's going on here?"

Back came the reply. "Stand back boss. You never know when that thing's going to start!"

Martha and Ramsay Sykes, Coylton

TWELVE

A hill walker was thirsty and coming across a hill burn decided to have a drink. The farmer saw him and shouted, "Dinna drink the waater its fu o' coo's sharn an p**h!"

The walker replies: "My good fellow, I'm from England. Could you repeat that for me in English?"

The farmer replied: "I said, use two hands - you'll spill less that way!"

Colin Blair, Darwin

Two farming friends went to the Royal Smithfield Show in London. One was married and the other a bachelor. They met this rather attractive young widow in a bar and finished back at her flat at which point the bachelor fell asleep. The next thing he remembers is his married pal shaking him awake: "Come on, let's get the hell oot o' here," he said. Nothing more was said about it until some nine months later, a telegram arrived for the bachelor from London. He read it with amazement and immediately jumped into his car to see his married friend. "Thon nicht in London," he said. "Fit happened when I fell asleep and you were left wi thon widow woman?" "Well," said his pal "We dimmed the lichts, pit on some music and, ye ken, ae thing led to anither." To which the bachelor enquired: "You didnae by ony chance give her my name, did ye?" "Well," his married pal replied. "Since I'm a married man and you're a bachelor, when she asked, I did give her your name. There's nothing wrang is there?."

"Na, na," said the bachelor. "There's nothing wrang. It's jist that I've had a telegram this mornin' fae London and she's left me a' her money!"

Eddie Gillanders, Farm North East

An old farmer was told by his doctor to go to his local hospital and give them a urine sample. On arriving there he was escorted to a fairly large room. A nurse soon arrived from the door opposite with a glass beaker in her hand and said to the farmer she needed a urine sample. He immediately unbuttoned his trousers, and as the nurse was four yards away asked, "Frae here?"

Colin Blair, Darwin

An Irishman was coming home from market with a sack on his back when he met an old friend.

"What have you got there?" asked the friend.

"Pigs. If you can guess how many there are in the bag, you can have both of them."

"Three," said the friend

Anon

One of the questions on the old forms that had to be filled in for an insurance claim following a car accident was "Is there any way this accident could have been avoided?" One Fife farmer responded by stating, "I suppose I could have gone by bus." The forms are no longer required.

Lynn Oliver, NFU Office, Cupar.

Two farm workers who were fed up with hoeing neeps decided to apply for jobs as butlers. When they went for interview they were told that they would have to wear kilts and that it would be necessary to look at their knees, feet and testimonials. As they left one said to the other "You know, I think if we had been better educated we would have got the jobs."

George Burgher, formerly Orkney & Shetland NFUS secretary

An old farmer hears a loud knock at his door. He opens the door and, to his amazement, standing there is a scantily clad young woman, who asks him, "Would you like super sex?" The old farmer stops, thinks for a minute, and responds, " I'll hae the soup."

Ian Williams, Campbell Dallas, Perth

Two old shepherds who met on the hill while looking after their sheep decided to have their tea together. One produced a Thermos flask. The other one looked at it and said, "Whit's this you have got, Angus?"

"Well," came the reply, "it's a thing called a Thermos flask."

"Oh, and what does that do?"

"Well, it keeps hot things hot and cold things cold."

"And what have you got in it the day?"

"The day I've a cup of coffee and two Ice lollies!"

Martha and Ramsay Sykes, Coylton

Jock says, "Tam, I'm thinking of buying a Labrador."

"Sod that," says Tam. "Have you seen how many of their owners go blind?"

Iain McCrone, Cardsknolls

This story concerns mud student, Willie who was one of those youngsters who grew up in the countryside and dreamed about becoming a farmer although he wasn't a farmer's son.

He used to help out on the farm on his holidays and managed to get a place in the Edinburgh College of Agriculture to study an HND .

He informed his childhood employers he would be doing a pre entry year's practical on a large cereal farm in Roxburghshire so he wouldn't be around for the upcoming harvest.

He said his farewells and set off for a year in the Borders only to return one week later to ask if he could resume his old post.

"What happened then Willie?" This was the question everyone in the tractor shed was eager to ask.

It was revealed that when young Willie arrived to take over from his predecessor, he was taken along to the local show dance as was the tradition.

After a few beers he was instructed to put on a tupping harness which he

did without question as he was eager to impress.

The older students then told him on request he was to simulate the art of tupping on a young lady of their choice.

Just at that, a young lady in a lovely white frock bent over to pick up her hand bag. "Her" went up the cry.

Willie was off and started to keel this young dame, unfortunately her father had spotted the sire at work and set upon him as he saw his daughter's now bright red rump.

Monday morning came and Willie reported for work bright and early and eager to impress but as the farmer whom he had not yet met turned up to

start the men. After a few beers he was instructed to put on a tupping harness which he did without question as he was eager to impress.

The older students then told him on request he was to simulate the art of tupping on a young lady of their choice.

Just at that, a young lady in a lovely white frock bent over to pick up her hand bag. "Her" went up the cry.

Willie was off and started to keel this young dame, unfortunately her father had spotted the sire at work and set upon him as he saw his daughter's now bright red rump.

Monday morning came and Willie reported for work bright and early and eager to impress but as the farmer whom he had not yet met turned up to start the men, Willie knew his time in the Borders was over.

Yes it was the father of the girl with bright red rear.

Murdo Fraser, Pitcairlie

Three farmers went to the Moscow Olympic games and to save money they decided to enter by the athletes' gateway.

The Scottish farmer took a clothes pole pretending that he was a pole vaulter.

The English farmer took a dustbin lid pretending to be a discus thrower.

The Irish farmer took a coil of barbed wire - he pretended to be a fencer.

George Burgher, formerly Orkney & Shetland NFUS secretary

Two stalwarts of the Wigtown Area NFU were Dougie McCrone and Moray Rhind. Both were heavy smokers and as the night wore on, business was often conducted through a haze of smoke. Eligibility for the then Sheep Annual Premium was dependent on retaining ewes for a qualifying period which happened one year to coincide with the holy period of Ramadan. Mutton was in big demand in that period but if you sold ewes in the retention period you forfeited your subsidy. Dougie therefore proposed, supported by Moray, that Headquarters' support was sought to change the timing of Ramadan. The Union has had its share of success but changing a major religious event for Muslims across the world was beyond it and the motion was not carried.

John Ross, Auchenree

An old Beef Shorthorn cattleman was introduced to the Queen Mother at the Royal Highland Show and he had a long conversation with her. One of the Press and Journal's team of reporters at the show, Ethel Simpson, rushed up to him afterwards, desperate to get a good local angle to the story. She asked him what he had said to the Queen Mother, "Och," he said. "I jist asked her fit she was daein' the nicht!"

Eddie Gillanders Farm North East

A crop research scientist with a reputation for insisting on absolute proof of any scientific work was travelling with a colleague. They passed a field of sheep and the colleague said 'I see Mains has sheared his sheep.'

"Hmm," said his passenger. "At least on one side."

Fordyce Maxwell, formerly Scotsman

The arrival of Artificial Insemination brought with it a wealth of stories including the first arrival of an AI man to the small Kincardineshire farm. Buttercup, the farm milk cow, was tethered and normally she was docile but this new way of doing things upset her and she kicked out against the intruder.

"You did not tell me, she was wild," complained the AI man as he nursed his bruised shins.

"She has never been bulled by a man in white overalls before," replied the farmer.

Anon

Two shepherds met three days after a long, hard-drinking, shepherds' supper.

"God," said one, "what a night that was. I ended up in jail."

"You were lucky," said his friend. "I got home."

Fordyce Maxwell, formerly Scotsman

A well known farmer on the outskirts of Perth brought a contractor in to sow his grain fields. When the crop came through the ground, the mess, which was right by the roadside, was obvious to all. There were great big missed bits right through the fields.

Mischievously, a neighbour phoned. "Rob, I am looking for some barley and I hear that you have some left over."

Anon

Wee Johnny was late for primary school... again.

It happened a lot because money was tight on the farm and his parents couldn't afford to employ a farm worker. The result was that the boy had lots of chores to do before he went to school.

The teacher was getting heartily fed up with the situation, so the next time Johnny tried to slip into the classroom late the teacher fumed at him angrily.

"Well James, what is it this time, that's made you so late?"

"Please miss, I haud tae tak the bull doon the road a pit him in the fiel' wi' the coos cos yin o them was abullin'."

"This is simply not good enough James. Could your father not have done that?"

Johnny took a moment to think and replied.

"Naw miss, Ah think it haes tae be the bull."

Neale McQuistin Airyolland

The local vet and doctor were good friends but had disagreements about who had the easier job, with the vet saying his job was harder as is patients couldn't speak.

One day the vet took ill and called his friend, the doctor, to attend to him.

The doctor asked him where he had pain. "Moo, moo" said the vet.

Again the doctor asked where had pain and the vet replied with a "miaow, miaow".

For a third time the doctor asked where it hurt and the vet replied this time with an "oink, oink".

So the doctor wrote out a prescription and gave it to the vet's wife.

When she collected the prescription from the chemist the box of pills had written on it "Take two tablets three times daily. If after a week there is no improvement, take to slaughterhouse."

Anne MacAskill

A Fife farmer was so bothered with pigeons eating his oilseed rape crop that he decided to invest in a gas banger. Off he went to Cupar and bought a gleaming new machine. Setting it up, he realised there were no set of instructions so he phoned the dealer. "Just fix it to a gas container," he was told. This he did and sure enough, the machine went off with a big bang followed by bits of paper floating down.

Picking them up, the farmer realised the scraps of paper were all that were left of the instruction manual and to add insult to injury, while the advice was there in German and French, the English version had been shot to pieces.

Campbell Brunton, Balmonth

An old codger, who had been a retired farmer for a long time, became very bored and decided to open a medical clinic.

He put a sign up outside that said: Dr. Codger's clinic. "Get your treatment for £500, if not cured get back £1,000."

Doctor Young who was positive that this old codger didn't know anything about medicine, thought this would be a great opportunity to get £1,000.

So he went to Dr. Codger's clinic.

Dr. Young: "Dr. Codger, I have lost all taste in my mouth" can you please help me?"

Dr. Codger: "Nurse, please bring medicine from box 22 and put 3 drops in Dr. Young's mouth."

Dr. Young: "Aaagh that was petrol!"

Dr. Codger: "Congratulations! You've got your taste back. That will be £500."

Dr. Young was annoyed and went back after a couple of days intending to recover his money.

Dr Young: "I've lost my memory, I cannot remember anything."

Dr. Codger: "Nurse, please bring medicine from box 22 and put 3 drops in the patient's mouth."

Doctor Young: "Oh no you don't. That is petrol!"

Dr. Codger: "Congratulations! You've got your memory back. That will be £500."

Dr. Young after having lost £1,000 left angrily but came back after several more days.

Dr. Young: "My eyesight has become weak I can hardly see!"

Dr. Codger: "Well, I don't have any medicine for that so here's your £1000 back."

Dr. Young: "But this is only £500."

Dr. Codger: "Congratulations! You got your sight back! That will be £500."

Dave Balfour, Auchtermuchty

Some young farmers visited Edinburgh and went out for an evening that they will never forget and ended up with a night that they could not remember.

George Burgher, formerly NFUS Orkney & Shetland

A farmer drove to his neighbour's house and knocked on the door. A small boy answered it. "Is your mum or dad in?" the farmer asked.

"No they went to town," said the boy.

"How about your brother, Bill is he here?"

"No he went with them," came the reply. Then he added, "I can give them a message if you want."

"Well," said the farmer rather uncomfortably, "I really want to talk to your dad about your brother getting my daughter Susie pregnant."

The boy thought for a moment, then said, "Yes you are right. You will have to talk to dad about that. I know he charges £300 for the bull and £100 for the tup but I have no idea how much he charges for Bill."

Jim Webster, Dunkeld

My predecessor told me of a visit he made to Friarton Farm, Newport on Tay in the late 1950s where he accompanied the farmer, Harry Adamson, over several grain fields. In each he advised, "Four pints of MCPA" only to be countered by the farmer's son, Andrew, who muttered "Three pints would do."

After several repetitions of this, the father took matters in hand by stating, "The firm is still H. Adamson & Son and not Son & H. Adamson. We'll be wanting four pints per acre."

Sandy Millar, consultant formerly SAI

THIRTEEN

Hugh Smith's family farmed in Kenya but he was sent back to the old country to learn about agriculture. During a lecture on animal husbandry we were being told about the perils of liver fluke in sheep. The fluke's other host was the mud snail which lived in wet, boggy parts. One method of prevention, the lecturer intoned, was to fence off the boggy areas in fields. Undeterred, the bold Hugh, one of life's contrarians/lateral thinkers asked in mock innocence, "Would the snails not get through the fence?"

Stanley Bayne, Gospetry

Farmer, looking enviously at new grandson: "All he has to do is eat, sleep and s**t - my ambition all my life."

Fordyce Maxwell, formerly Scotsman

"How did it happen?" said the doctor as he was setting the broken leg of a farm worker. "Well, doctor," said the man, "Twenty five years ago when I started to work on the farm, that first night, after I had gone to bed the beautiful farmer's daughter came into my room. She asked me if there was anything that I wanted. Are you sure she said. Isn't there anything that I can do for you?" "What has that got to do with you broken leg?" "Well doctor, this morning when it dawned on me what she meant, I fell off the roof."

George Burgher, former Orkney & Shetland NFUS secretary

Jim Lawrie took his brand new mobility scooter to Kinross Show and was soon going round the stands enjoying the hospitality. By mid afternoon, he was well refreshed but could not find his wife to drive him home in the car.

Undeterred, he set sail in his new form of transport and made his way through both Kinross and Milnathort before he was tracked down and firmly told to get into the car.

George Lawrie, NFUS treasurer

Food plays a big part in the life of a farming journalist, eating it that is. Most of the time, it's a good experience, but not always.

My most negative experience involved visiting a livestock farm in Ayrshire, a place where the family basically did a bit of everything; cattle, sheep, a few pigs and some poultry.

The interview had gone well and I was just about ready to leave when the farmer's wife suggested a plate of bacon and eggs before I left. There were a couple of kids in the kitchen, who had maybe not seen soap and water for a few days, and the place itself was less than spotless. My own farming background had carried a certain rustic edge to it, however, so I accepted the offer of food with a degree of enthusiasm. What came next, however, forced me to invent an urgent, and previously forgotten meeting, long before you could ever press the recall button on your mobile phone and blame your sudden change of mind on some faceless editor.

"Run to the pig house and get the frying pan," said the wife, dispatching the least clean child to complete the task. "They've been scouring and I gave them something for it this morning."

I took this to mean the pigs, not the kids. Whichever it was, I could see a dining rethink was becoming urgent.

I impressed myself by actually waiting until the frying pan returned to kitchen, only making my excuses when the scour-fresh pan was slapped straight onto the kitchen stove.

Colin Ley

Visiting the West coast of Scotland in the middle of a wet summer the tourist asked one of the locals how often it rained. "Only twice last week; once for three days and the other time for four."

Anon

During the Troubles, an Irish farmer found a sandwich in his field and it had two wires in it. He phoned the police who asked if it was a bomb and if it was ticking. "No," said the Irishman, "I had a look inside and I think it is ham."

Jim Webster, Dunkeld

Members of Ayr Area of the NFUS were often of an independent mind and feared no one. On one visit, President John Ross remarked that he would have preferred to have the then United Nations Secretary General, Boutros Boutros-Gahli accompanying him.

Howard Jefferson, former NFUS Ayr

The farmer and his wife were out for a run in their car and, like all farmers, he was rubber necking to see how all his neighbours' crops and stock were looking; all the time paying minimal attention to the road.

Suddenly, he asked his wife, "What height is a penguin?"

"About three feet, why do you ask?"

"In that case, I have just run over a nun."

Peter Small, Falfield

A farmer's wife was granted a divorce because every time that there was lightning he jumped out of bed and shouted, "I'll buy the negatives."

(For younger readers, this was before digital cameras arrived and did away with the need for film.)

George Burgher, former Orkney & Shetland NFUS secretary

Cow Definitions:

SOCIALISM
You have 2 cows.
You give one to your neighbour.

COMMUNISM
You have 2 cows.
The State takes both and gives you some milk.

FASCISM
You have 2 cows.
The State takes both and sells you some milk.

BUREAUCRATISM
You have 2 cows.
The State takes both, shoots one, milks the other, and then throws the milk away.

TRADITIONAL CAPITALISM
You have two cows.
You sell one and buy a bull. Your herd multiplies, and the economy grows. You sell them and retire on the income.

VENTURE CAPITALISM
You have two cows.
You sell three of them to your publicly listed company, using letters of credit opened by your brother-in-law at the bank, then execute a debt/equity swap with an associated general offer so that you get all four cows back, with a tax exemption for five cows. The milk rights of the six cows are transferred via an intermediary to a Cayman Island Company secretly owned by the majority shareholder who sells the rights to all seven cows back to your listed company. The annual report says the company owns eight cows, with an option on one more. You sell one cow to buy a new

president of the United States, leaving you with nine cows. No balance sheet provided with the release. The public then buys your bull.

SURREALISM
You have two giraffes.
The government requires you to take harmonica lessons.

AN AMERICAN CORPORATION
You have two cows.
You sell one, and force the other to produce the milk of four cows. Later, you hire a consultant to analyse why the cow has dropped dead.

A FRENCH CORPORATION
You have two cows.
You go on strike, organise a riot, and block the roads, because you want three cows.

A JAPANESE CORPORATION
You have two cows.
You redesign them so they are one-tenth the size of an ordinary cow and produce twenty times the milk. You then create a clever cow cartoon image called a Cowkimona and market it worldwide.

AN ITALIAN CORPORATION
You have two cows, but you don't know where they are.
You decide to have lunch.

A SWISS CORPORATION
You have 5000 cows. None of them belong to you.
You charge the owners for storing them.

A CHINESE CORPORATION
You have two cows.
You have 300 people milking them. You claim that you have full

employment, and high bovine productivity. You arrest the newsman who reported the real situation.

AN INDIAN CORPORATION
You have two cows.
You worship them.

A BRITISH CORPORATION
You have two cows.
Both are mad.

AN IRAQI CORPORATION
Everyone thinks you have lots of cows.
You tell them that you have none. No-one believes you, so they bomb the ** out of you and invade your country. You still have no cows, but at least you are now a Democracy.

AN AUSTRALIAN CORPORATION
You have two cows.
Business seems pretty good. You close the office and go for a few beers to celebrate.

A NEW ZEALAND CORPORATION
You have two cows.
The one on the left looks very attractive.

Erika Hay, Perth